Cancer. Alzheimers. F ⬛⬛⬛ g. In *Aging
Grace,* Dr. Caracciolo ⬛⬛⬛ ⬛dation for
hope in the midst of t ⬛⬛⬛ ill face this
side of heaven.

> —Dr. Tim Clinton
> President, American Association of Christian
> Counselors

I have known Dr. Rick for several years. His passion for the aging is so deeply rooted in who he is that it is contagious. A few minutes with Dr. Rick and you will soon understand the depth of his passion and the wealth of knowledge he has on the subject. He is not only a caring individual, but truly desires to provide practical learning for both the aging and those who care for the aging. His heart is to instill a respect for the aging in our generation. *Aging Grace* is a must read for those who have aging parents and/or loved ones who are reaching the point in their lives where a little help from someone who reads this book will prolong their independence and strengthen their dignity. I am convinced that *Aging Grace* will have lasting impact on ensuring that aging doesn't have to equate to a burdensome dependence.

> —Dave Divine
> Pastor, The Church at Chapel Hill
> Douglasville, GA
> www.churchatchapelhill.com

A practical guide for everyone who still has their parents—each area is thoughtfully presented with common sense, yet easily read for all parties involved. This is pure ministry to the body of Christ—in everyday living by having the broad scope that is covered with the data, images, and research by a professional who serves others. This book is one that should be purchased, read, and applied in every home where parents are still living in preparation for a time of aging gracefully...

> —Rev. Michael G. "Moe" Bruner

Easy read. Once I started, I wanted to finish. I would recommend *Aging Grace* for basic reading for Christian counselors working with our aging citizens.

—Joanne Willis, OTR/L
Occupational Therapist
Executive Director, Touch The Future, Inc.,
www.touchthefuture.us

It's really great that the chapters help to show that aging should not be viewed as a negative, but as a time that God can use a person for great things. A very good resource for a care taker, and at a time that can be one of the most trying. Hopefully this book will help someone collect all the information one needs without having to scramble to look in a million different places. I recommend *Aging Grace* to anyone responsible for the care of an aging individual.

—Misty Davis, OTR/L
Occupational Therapist
Long Term Care

It was an honor and privilege to be the live-in care-giver of my Godly mother for the last several years of her life. She was very patient and daily she lived the life she told others about, which made it easy to care for her. We had to learn many things the hard way—by trial and error. This book would have been a big help. Christian counselors and care-givers will benefit from reading *Aging Grace* and keeping it in their library for future reference.

—Mary McPherson
Care-giver, Baby Boomer and Retired Principal

Aging Grace

Advice for Pastors, Counselors, and Families of Aging Relatives

Aging Grace

Advice for Pastors, Counselors, and Families of Aging Relatives

Dr. Rick C. Caracciolo

HIGHERLIFE
DEVELOPMENT SERVICES, INC

Oviedo, Florida

Aging Grace—Advice for Pastors, Counselors, and Families of Aging Relatives
by Rick C. Caracciolo

Published by HigherLife Development Services, Inc.
400 Fontana Circle
Building 1, Suite 105
Oviedo, Florida 32765
(407) 563-4806
www.ahigherlife.com

Cover Design: Tracy Jetté

Photos of assistive devices provided by Maxi-Aids Inc. Available at www.maxiaids.com or by calling toll-free at 1-800-522-6294. Free catalogs available with over 244 pages filled with helpful items.

First Edition
09 10 11 12 13 — 8 7 6 5 4 3 2 1
Printed in the United States of America

Dedication

My prayer is that you learn, apply the truths, and are blessed from reading this book. Without God there would be nothing. He has put me on a path that has been phenomenal. I have been given the opportunity to learn academically and work hands on in the physical, spiritual, and psychological arenas. I have seen excellent care-giver's first hand—my parents, Marguerite—my wife and others with whom I have worked. I will not get the privilege to be a care-giver for my parents because by man's standards they unexpectedly passed early in life (but God's timing was then so they could spend extra time with Him). It is a privilege to be a care-giver and care receiver. It will probably be one of the hardest things you will ever do, but it can also be one of the most rewarding.

Just as millions of other Baby Boomers, I have a vested interest in the future. I now have the opportunity to share my experiences and what I have learned.

I am blessed by the passion put on my heart and the opportunity to meet and work with such caring people. Also the team at HigherLife; thanks for everyone's suggestions, editing, and insights—they have been great.

Thanks Mom and Dad.

Table of Contents

Foreword

Growing older brings many challenges. Too many people travel in that journey alone. We hope to change that. Support and encouragement are available for aging men and women who are facing significant life-changing experiences. Family members, professional care-givers, and licensed counselors can all benefit from these resources.

Aging Grace outlines the resources, options, and information available for counselors to present to family members or the responsible parties committed to helping people face the realities of decreased independence due to aging. This is especially helpful when an older person has become unable to live safely at home alone.

Christian counselors are trained to help individuals in the spiritual and mental health arenas, but counseling the elderly and their families is a whole new dimension for many of them. The concerns and afflictions are also physical (physiological) in nature—an area of health care in which most counselors have limited training and familiarity. Without attempting to replace those who are specialists in physical disabilities, it is my intent to inform, educate, and provide resources for the aging, their care-givers, and counselors so that we can all be more knowledgeable and communicate effectively with each other and with health care providers who specialize in physical infirmities and disabilities. This makes it possible for us all to better assist the whole person—the spiritual, physical, and mental needs of an aging person, his or her care-givers, and their loved ones.

As human beings—many of us Brothers and Sisters in Christ—we are all experiencing the aging process in our own ways. We are all in our own unique positions with a great purpose—to give and receive grace as we help each other through all of the days ordained for each of us as we seek to see needs, serve people, and solve challenges with "an aging grace."

—Dr. Rick

Chapter 1

GRACEFUL AGING
Seeing the Situation Clearly

Seeing the Aging Process for What It Is and How It Affects Us All

For each of us, the aging process is taking its unique toll on our physical, financial, emotional, relational, and spiritual resources. We all need to face these challenges and make the necessary adjustments with the highest possible levels of hopefulness, humility, and concern for personal dignity. As loving care-givers, we never know when an emergency or urgent need will arise and require our most empathetic, compassionate, and expert intervention. Counselors never know when an issue of aging will become a crisis situation for a person or a person's loved ones. We need to be prepared when called upon to counsel, assist, or provide information related to aging.

As the elderly population grows, individuals and families will need assistance to find resources, available options and help in locating and previewing suitable care facilities when an aging family member is unable to live at home alone. Not being able to live alone safely does not mean that the individual will have to move out of their residence. We are defining unable to live at home alone as, "not being able to live at home alone safely without assistance." This does not mean that a care-giver or family member cannot stop by to give assistance or even live in full-time. This is a broad definition because each individual's health and family circumstances will be different and unique to that person so a broad definition is required.

What can a Christian counselor know in order to counsel the elderly and their family members competently when a family member can no longer live safely at home alone? This type of counseling situation is one that can bring about a tremendous amount of stress, anxiety, and anger for all of those involved if the situation is not handled properly.

Seeing Ourselves for What We're Made of ... and More!

The human body that was created by God is nothing less than miraculous. God has designed our unmatchable human bodies with hundreds of bones, miles of blood vessels, and trillions of cells, all of which are constantly working together and performing all kinds of different functions. We are delicate and resilient, weak and strong, dynamic and static, happy and sad, or growing and dormant—that is the human body. According to the Agency for Healthcare Research and Quality (AHRQ) AHCPR Research on Long-term Care, statistics show that 4 out of every 10 people turning 65 will have the need of part or full-time nursing care at some point in their lives. As our population ages, the demand for these services will only continue to grow. To aid families, the Christian counselor will need to have an understanding of what is involved physically, emotionally, spiritually, and financially in finding acceptable options, care facilities within a convenient distance, and also supply our clients with up-to-date resources for families to have a successful outcome and a positive effect.

In 1999, Baby Boomers represented almost 30 percent of the U.S. population. Over the next 12 to 30 years, they'll age to 65 or older. That means that by 2030, one in every five Americans will be at least 65 years of age. That statistic, combined with the longevity in this country, greatly magnifies the importance of finding quality resources and optional services.[1]

God created man in His own image; we are fearfully and wonderfully made. God made each and every one of us unique individuals. We have different skin colors, hair colors, body shapes, and sizes. But we are all God's children. God knew who we were even before we were born. Psalm 139:13 NIV says, "For you created my inmost being; you knit me together in my mother's womb." The human body is so intriguing and intricate that only a loving God could have created man. Man is the only species whose life span is known to expand decades past our reproductive years. What makes man so special? The main substance of the human body is water, accounting for 70 to 85 percent of the body's mass. At first glance the human body seems almost unimpressive because it is made up of water and a few simple chemicals.

- Carbon—A chemical also found in diamonds and coal. A fifth of our body is coal.
- Iron—Iron makes the blood red. The human body has enough iron to make a small nail.
- Phosphorus—This can be found in our bones and teeth.
- Sodium and Chlorine—These two chemicals make salt. The human body is 1/3 as salty as sea water.
- Potassium—This can be found in our bodily fluids. It is also used in some types of soap.
- Nitrogen—This chemical is important to muscles and is also the main ingredient in air.[2]

If our bodies were recycled and the metals extracted from our remains, we would be worth about ten dollars. We are more than singly listed elements, chemicals, and liquid. There are over 20 commonplace elements that can be found in the earth's dust (Genesis 3:19). In the body these elements are combined in so many different ways that we are actually made up of thousands upon thousands of complex chemical compounds. Even more remarkable is the fact that the human body is not just a static jumble of chemicals but a dynamic, highly organized, marvelous designed living organism. It constructs itself. It grows, acts and reacts, regulates its own activities, and keeps its parts in fairly good repair.[3]

The Cells and Skin

In the human body there are 75–100 trillion cells categorized into about 100 different types. About 50,000 tiny flakes of dead skin drop off our bodies every minute.[4] The average person has a total of 6 pounds of skin. The main job of the skin is to protect internal organs from drying up and to prevent harmful bacteria from getting inside.

The Nervous System

The human body has 93,200 miles of nerves throughout. The brain begins to lose thousands of neurons a day by age 30.[5] These cells are not replaced when they die and by the time we reach the age of 80 our brains will weigh about 7 percent less than they did in our prime. What does all of this mean? Mental skills and tasks become harder, reaction time increases, our perception of heat and cold decreases, and we find it harder to keep our balance.[6]

The Cardiovascular System

The heart loses about 1 percent of its reserve pumping capacity each year after the age of 30, reducing the amount of oxygen delivered throughout the body. The heart has 4 chambers and is about the size of a closed fist. It beats an average of 100-120 times a minute, 6,000 times in an hour, and 144,000 times a day.[7]

The Respiratory System

As our lungs age, they are no longer able to inflate or deflate completely because they have become less elastic. Our left lung is smaller than our right lung to allow room for the heart. We take about 23,000 breaths each day.[8]

The Musculoskeletal System

There are 206 bones in the body and about 650 of our muscles are wrapped around the bones of the skeleton.[9] The muscles in the average human body make up 40 percent of a body, its weight. Muscles can contract to 1/3 of their size. The muscles in our faces allow us to make 10,000 different facial expressions.[10] It takes seventeen facial muscles to smile and forty muscles to frown. The skeletal system continues to maintain and replace itself as long as specific cells work.

The osteoclast cells carry off old bone cells. The new cells are called osteoblast and they replace the old cells. The amount of new bone formed will depend upon the body's demands for skeletal support. When an individual is confined to bed or there is a decrease of physical activity, their skeletal and muscle strength usually declines. This is one reason that after an illness an individual might have difficulty doing activities they previously did before their illness. Muscle mass and strength decline as we age due to a loss of muscle fibers and the nerves that stimulate them. Men and women tend to lose bone mass as they age. This process usually begins earlier in women and proceeds more rapidly due to a reduction in estrogen levels as menopause nears.

The Digestive System

The digestive system holds up better than most of the other body systems. Like the muscular structures, the alimentary organs (esophagus, stomach, small intestine, and colon) lose tone with age. The regular contractions that propel food through them become less frequent, less speedy, and take longer to process it. The other digestive organs begin to slow with age also. The gallbladder becomes sluggish in releasing bile into the small intestine, increasing the probability of gallstones. The liver shrinks with age and receives a smaller blood supply and needs more time to metabolize food, drugs, and alcohol.

The Immune System

The immune system becomes hampered by the gradual degeneration of the thymus. The thymus is a small gland in the neck responsible for helping coordinate the body's defense system. This gland reaches its maximum size by puberty and then begins to shrink shortly after and virtually disappears by old age. This in turn leaves the immune system less resilient and capable of fighting off diseases and infections.

The Excretory System

As we get older, the kidneys begin to have a gradual reduction of blood flow along with a decrease in the nephrons (filtering units) which impairs their ability to extract waste from the blood and concentrate into urine. The kidneys will now require more water to excrete the same amount of waste as when we were younger. The capacity of the bladder also declines as we get older, which in turn requires us to urinate more often.

The Sensory System

The five senses also begin to diminish with age. The lens of the eye is not as elastic and is not able to change, focus, or redirect on objects as quickly—and in some instances not at all. The sense of taste decreases as the number of taste buds lessens. There are four different types of taste: bitter, sour, salty, and sweet. We become less able to appreciate a wide range of flavors and taste. Our sense of taste becomes less discriminating and our ability to distinguish different foods diminishes. The sense of smell decreases as we become more increasingly oblivious to delicate fragrances. The sense of hearing varies with each individual just as our vision does. The three bones in the ear are the smallest in the human body. The stapes is the smallest and is no larger than a grain of rice.

The Endocrine System

One of the main systems of the body for communicating, controlling, and coordinating the body's work is the endocrine system. The endocrine system works with the pancreas, kidneys, liver, reproductive system, stomach, nervous system, and fat in the body to help maintain and control of the following:

- body energy levels
- growth and development
- response to stress, environment, and injury
- homeostasis—internal balance of body systems

This is accomplished by the endocrine system through a network of glands and organs that produce, store, and secrete particular types of hormones. Different types of hormones will cause different effects on other cells or tissues of the body. The hormone secreting glands shrink as we get older, but their performance seems not to be as affected. Age alone does not change the output of the thyroid hormone, which regulates metabolism. Adrenalin, which coordinates the body's response to stress or pituitary hormones stimulates the thyroid, adrenal glands, and ovaries. The aging pancreas secretes insulin to regulate glucose metabolism and can respond to sudden increases in blood sugar.[11]

If all of our systems declined at the same time the outlook would be pretty bleak. Each system ages according to its own timetable and this can vary quite dramatically from person to person. Some of the factors that affect the timetable are genetics, lifestyle, and personal well being. The human body is fearfully and wonderfully made.

The average life expectancy has been increasing significantly from thirty-seven years old in 1776, forty-seven years old in 1900 to seventy-nine years old in 2000.[12] This is only the average life expectancy. A woman who lives to sixty-five years of age generally has another eighteen years life expectancy and a female who lives to be eighty-five years old averages another six years of life expectancy. Aging, like the future, has no predictable pattern. Some aging experts and gerontologists believe that the human life span will not go much beyond eighty-five years of age if there are not any significant breakthroughs in the aging process. How realistic is it to believe that the aging process will stop?

We have no way of determining when life expectancy and the aging process will come to a standstill. "No one understands why we age, and there have been more than 300 theories proposed that have a connection to aging."[13] Old age is a mental attitude as well as a physical concern. Most people cringe in discussions about getting older. Through the ages people have tried numerous ways to postpone old age. They have tried various foods, products, drinks, and support groups. They have tried traveling to feel young and fulfilled. They apply creams, drink concoctions, follow charts, and enroll in so-called health programs to try and postpone their aging.

God has a plan for us. It is bigger than any problem life can produce. God's plan is that old age be the crowning glory of a person's lifetime. The Word of God shows that old age can have promise, productivity, vitality, confidence, and happiness. How? When spiritual preparation has taken place during the younger years. Many individuals become old before their time because they have spent too much time worrying about being prepared for old age and concentrating on how to prevent problems—many of which they have no control over as they get older.

There are a number of key terms and concepts to know when addressing health care concerns. A glossary is included in Appendix A later in this book (page 131). A number of abbreviations and acronyms are also noted and explained there.

Seeing What the Experts Say about Aging

The age group of those eighty-five and older is the fastest-growing segment of the American population today. In fact, the number of people belonging to this group has more than tripled since 1970. "As more and more of us are living into these later years, we're more likely to experience chronic illnesses, disabilities, and dependency."[14] In locating, recognizing, and compiling quality resources it will be possible to alleviate some of the complications involved in finding a variety of resources when asked to counsel individuals or family members on this subject.

In most instances when we are asked for help or advice on this topic, it is an emergency situation and those involved do not have a significant amount of time to make a decision. There are approximately 17,000 nursing homes and approximately 30,000 assisted living residences in the United States.[15] Currently accurate figures are not available as to the number of individuals who are living at home with assistance. It helps to be able to narrow down the number of choices to those facilities and other options that meet the counselee's general guidelines and specific concerns they might have for their situation.

Aging is Natural—Not the Enemy

Mankind's resistance to the process of aging has probably not changed dramatically since the beginning of time 2,000 years ago, or over the last 220 years as man's life expectancy has increased. "Psychologists tell us that all of life is made up of continuous changes from childhood all the way to old age."[16] The last twenty years of life, the stage we call old age, brings about almost as many changes as the first twenty years. These changes carry the threat of loss, disability, and other degenerative conditions.[17]

Christian counselors are generally trained in the spiritual and mental health aspects. As the graying of America continues at an accelerated rate, the Christian counselor is going to need the tools and resources to counsel in this area. Aging affects everyone. The Christian counselor can benefit not only his clients, but also himself professionally and personally by having an understanding of aging, dealing with physical disabilities, and the intricacy of the human body. Also having the knowledge of where to retrieve additional updated information for a client is a blessing to all. It helps reassure the counselee during a stressful time that there is someone who cares and is trying to help. Also, caregivers and counselors who gain these skills and acquire this knowledge will be better equipped to truly serve the whole person—in the spiritual, mental, and physical dimensions.

Again, not every family member or counselor needs to become a specialist in aging or a gerontologist. The expectation is that we can at least become a resource for those in need or can refer clients to a Christian counselor who specializes in the area of aging issues and concerns.

Gracious Living—A Spiritual Perspective

Some biblical scholars believe Scriptures indicate that there are three broad divisions of a lifetime. The period of youth lasts up to the age of forty. When Moses was around forty he began to sense his responsibility to Israel and to the Lord (Acts 7:23). Moses spent forty more years in training before he became the leader to the people of Israel. Moses did his great works during the years from eighty to 120.

Paul writes in 1 Timothy 4:12, "Let no man despise thy youth." Timothy is thought to have been a man in his 30s at the time this letter was written. A man was healed and the Sanhedrin wanted to ridicule his testimony. In Acts 4:22, we find "the man was above forty years on whom this healing was shown," indicating he was mature enough to know what had happened.

The years of age from forty to sixty are considered the middle-age period. Many believers accomplish a significant amount in the middle years. A sixty-year-old widow's retirement was turned into a full-time ministry of prayer supported by the church (1 Timothy 5:9). The high priest workload was at its heaviest between the ages of thirty and fifty.

The period of old age was from sixty years and on. At the age of ninety, Daniel was told to stop acting like a dead man and get going. A woman eighty-four years old was very active in serving the Lord (Luke 2:36-38).

Some of the most unhappy and miserable elderly people call themselves Christians. They are grumpy, demanding, and obnoxious. They no longer have their youth to hide behind and protect them. They are now out in the open for all to see. Proverbs 23:7 so wisely says, "As a man thinks in his heart so is he." Their youthfulness has been the excuse for bad behavior; now they don't have that argument to hide behind. Exposed by old age, all of their faults, habits, and characteristics are on display. King Solomon wrote Ecclesiastes when he reached "old age." He had some advice for the young to adhere to so they could prevent heartaches in their later years: "Find happiness when you are young." However, at any age, we can carry inner happiness from the Word of God, which does not depend upon conditions or circumstances within or around us, creating a fulfilling old age.

Gracious Living—A Mind at Work

In *Man's Search for Meaning*, Viktor E. Frankl concluded that those who survive are those who make meaning from their situations, who find activities that give purpose even in the most hopeless circumstances. He emphasized the necessity of finding meaning in life no matter what life involves.[18] While an activity might be similar from one person to another, the meaning of the activity will differ based on the characteristics of the individual, background, circumstances, and religious beliefs.

Gracious Living—A Body of Energy

Why does exercise help us to live longer? There are two main reasons. First, exercise helps the body resist disease triggered by priming the immune system, those cells that protect against disease. Also, exercise improves blood circulation keeping the body and brain in good condition and helping to resist primary aging.[19] An advocate for staying active in the later years, Dr. Josef P. Hrachovec says, "Exercise is the closest thing to an anti-aging pill now available. It acts like a miracle and it's free for the doing."[20] Research has shown us that physical activity is beneficial for the health of people at any age, including those sixty-five and over.

Physical activity can reduce the risk of certain chronic diseases, relieve symptoms of depression, help to maintain independent living, and enhance overall quality of life. Scientific research has shown that even among the frail and very old adults, mobility and functioning can be improved through physical activity.

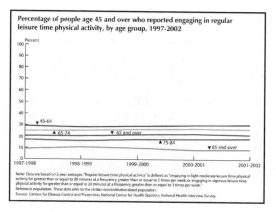

Percentage of people age 45 and over who reported engaging in regular leisure time physical activity, by age group, 1997-2002

Note: Data are based on 2-year averages. "Regular leisure time physical activity" is defined as "engaging in light-moderate leisure time physical activity for greater than or equal to 30 minutes at a frequency greater than or equal to 5 times per week, or engaging in vigorous leisure time physical activity for greater than or equal to 20 minutes at a frequency greater than or equal to 3 times per week."
Reference population: These data refer to the civilian noninstitutionalized population.
Source: Centers for Disease Control and Prevention, National Center for Health Statistics, National Health Interview Survey.

The percentage of people sixty and older engaging in regular leisure time physical activity was 21 percent in 2001–2002. Men over sixty-five were more likely than women in the same age group to report being involved in some type of regular physical activity.

There are several other types of physical activity that contribute to overall health and fitness. Strength training has been recommended as part of a comprehensive physical activity program among older adults and may help to improve balance and decrease risk of falls.

What can be done to help prevent or delay the onset of chronic diseases such as coronary heart disease, certain types of cancer, stroke, and Type 2 diabetes? An improvement in dietary quality. A healthy diet can reduce some major risk factors for chronic diseases, such as obesity, high blood pressure, and high cholesterol.[21]

The Gift of Community—Sharing the Burden to Meet the Need

Senior centers began in the United States in the early 1940s. Today, there are between 10,000 and 12,000 centers in the United States. A vast majority of the senior centers are multipurpose and offer a wide range of health, social, recreational, and educational services. The Older Americans Act (OAA) has focused on these types of centers to serve as community focal points for comprehensive service coordination and delivery at the local level. Senior centers provide services for seniors and are focal points in providing important information and referrals through connections with a variety of organizations as well as participation with local, state, and government programs. These centers are often used by other agencies as delivery centers for programs such as congregate meals and health education.[22]

The larger senior centers usually have paid staff and rely on volunteers also to assist. Research suggests that users of these senior centers generally have higher levels of health, social interaction, and life satisfaction, though they generally have lower levels of income than non-users. Many of the senior centers in the larger cities, suburbs, and rural areas are facing challenges and opportunities associated with the increasing numbers of seniors from diverse ethnic backgrounds.[23]

In *Advance Care Planning: Preference for Care at the End of Life*, L. Bucher says many seniors and their families are confused because of the lack of easy access to relevant, publicly communicated information and misunderstandings of the aging and disease process.[24] This in turn causes additional turmoil and stress for individuals, families, and care-givers. Many individuals continue to struggle alone with their problems not knowing which way to turn until forced to make a decision in a crisis or emergency situation with little or no information. Finding out how to qualify for and use available services is very important.

To Age or Not to Age? There is No Question

Americans are living longer than ever before. The growth of the population of those sixty-five and over affects many aspects of our society, challenging policymakers, families, businesses, and health care providers (among others) to meet the needs of aging individuals. During the 20th century, the older population grew from three million to thirty-five million. In 2003, nearly thirty-six million people age sixty-five and over lived in the United States accounting for just over 12 percent of the population. The oldest population, those eighty-five and over, grew from just over 100,000 in 1900 to 4.2 million in 2000.[25]

We need to have a proper spiritual, historical, and cultural context for understanding the aging process, its social structures, and traditions and to know why they are important.

Mankind seems to have always had a view of immortality and has not wanted to face the fact that we get older. We cannot maintain our physical abilities. The question now is what does old age mean? The definition and perception of aging has changed and been redefined over the last 150 years. The changing of society and extended lifespan has contributed to the confusion about the expectations, performance, expected roles, and activities of older adults. This has come about in part because the United States at one time was primarily an agricultural society. Then we developed into an industrial society and now primarily are becoming a technological society. This has assisted in changing the experience of aging in the United States.[26]

Life expectancy is a summary of the overall health of a population. It represents the average number of years of life remaining to a person at a given age if death rates were to remain constant. In the United States, improvements in health have resulted in increased life expectancy and contributed to the growth of the older population over the past century.

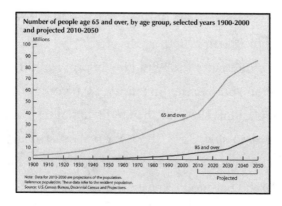

Number of people age 65 and over, by age group, selected years 1900-2000 and projected 2010-2050

A recent development is retirement. In years past, people rarely lived long enough to retire, and those who did often had ongoing responsibilities. As Achenbaum and Stern have stated, "We cannot discuss old age without some sense of trend, of where we are coming from and where we are heading."[27] Since life expectancy has increased significantly, man has even less of a tendency to accept the fact that he and his family should research and investigate potential options for emergency situations or their later years in life. If and when these services are needed, the individual and family members will feel more comfortable under pressure in making a decision if they are prepared.

Talking about Our Generations

The Baby Boomers, those born between 1946 and 1964, will be turning 65 in 2011. The number of older individuals will increase dramatically during the 2010-2030 period. The older population in 2030 is expected to be twice as large as their counterparts in 2000, growing from 35 million to 71.5 million and representing nearly 20 percent of the total U.S. population. The growth rate of the older population is projected to slow after 2030 when the last of the Baby Boomers enter the ranks of the older population. From the year 2030 and beyond, the proportion age sixty-five and over will be relatively stable at around 20 percent even though the absolute number of people age sixty-five and older is projected to continue to grow.[28]

The oldest segment of the population is projected to grow rapidly after 2030 when the Baby Boomers move into this age group. The United States Census Bureau projects that the population of those aged eighty-five and over could grow from 4.2 million in 2000 to nearly 21 million by 2050. Some researchers predict that death rates could decline in the older ages more rapidly than are reflected in the United States Census Bureau's projections, which could lead to a faster growth of this age group.

The proportion of the population age sixty-five and over varies by state. The population is partly affected by the state fertility and mortality levels and by the number of older and younger people who migrate to and from the state. The highest proportion of people age sixty-five and over in 2002 was Florida with 17 percent. Pennsylvania and West Virginia also had relatively high proportions of over 15 percent.[29]

The proportion of the population age sixty-five and over varies even more by county. In 2002, one county in North Dakota's population of sixty-five and over was 35 percent. In Florida, several counties had a proportion of over 30 percent. On the other end of the spectrum, in one county in Georgia, population was only 2 percent of those sixty-five and over.[30]

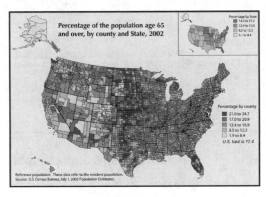

In most countries of the world, women outnumber men. The United States is no exception. The proportion that is female increases with age. In 2003, women accounted for 58 percent of the population age sixty-five and over and for 69 percent of the population age eighty-five and over.

The United States is fairly young for a developed country with just 12 percent of its population age sixty-five and over. The older population made up more than 15 percent of the population in most European countries and nearly 19 percent in both Italy and Japan.[31]

Functioning in later years may be diminished due to illness, chronic disease, mental disabilities, or an injury, which limits physical strength and mobility.

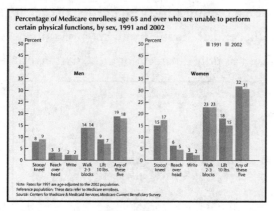

Older women (31 percent) reported more problems than men (18 percent) in regards to being unable to perform at least one of the five activities mentioned above. Physical functioning problems were more frequent at older ages. Physical functioning was related to race but not strongly. [32]

Considering Our Options

There are many factors, both internal and external, that affect the decisions that we make. Some of the internal factors that should be considered when making choices:

- an individual's preferences
- care-giver responsibilities
- cultural
- family dynamics
- individual's health condition.

Factors that are considered external influences when making decisions:

- location of health services
- housing options
- financial resources
- medical options
- health care provider availability.

Both internal factors and external factors will have an influence on the decision making process. When weighing all of the choices most importantly you should consider what is the best solution for the elderly. You can develop a workable plan that works for everyone involved. Each family member will have to determine what is important—not a personal desire—but what is required to meet current and future needs.

Categories and Contexts of Personal Preferences

Individual Preferences

Having to choose or modify a living arrangement is never easy. Of the 21.8 million households headed by older persons, 80 percent were owners and 20 percent were renters in 2001.[33] As individuals age, they generally require more assistance and become more dependent upon outside help and assistance. Each individual has a preference and lifestyle that they would like to maintain. Some individuals prefer to live alone where other individuals thrive on the company and assistance of others. The Baby Boomers seem to be in denial about their fast approaching golden years. They're putting forth very little effort to plan for their future. Robert Blancato who served as executive director for White House Conference on Aging in 1995 stated that he thinks the baby boomer suffers from what he calls the "three D" syndrome. They delay, deny, and demand. They have delayed the saving and planning for their senior years. They deny they are aging and demand action when they want something.[34]

Care-giver

This informal group of individuals has become one of the largest in the United States.[35] This group has similar life experiences, feelings, and attitudes. Many times care-givers feel alone, unappreciated, abandoned, and guilty about the situation they are involved in. Some care-givers have chosen to help out; others were chosen because of circumstances beyond their control. A care-giver can be a family member, an individual, or a company that provides personal assistance or services that the individual cannot perform themselves. Some of the other duties a care-giver could provide assistance in doing are grocery shopping, meal preparation, house cleaning, laundry, and medical appointments. Each individual and their families have their own set of circumstances to weigh such as the individual's health, finances, housing, and safety factors that make their decisions unique to them. In either situation, a network of support and assistance will be required. Each care-giving situation is different, but each individual goes through the same emotional roller coaster of feelings. "There is no normal. The key to coping and understanding a parent's or other aging loved one's changing needs is to learn to recognize actions and identify symptoms that fall outside of expected and acceptable changes."[36] As we age we change and it is often difficult for us to know when we are appreciated or might need to offer assistance. "In society our role is often through the emotions we experience as a parent, sibling, brother, sister, children, friend, and trusted adviser."[37] The loss of an identity can cause someone to feel lost and lonely. Care-giving isn't for the weak. Care-givers know the individual that they are caring for and have to be honest about the situation. Is it manageable? Will help be required? Family members who become care-givers must realize they need help and assistance. They should set up a network before beginning initial care for the individual. They should look for:

- Respite care so they can take a regular break.

- Help to assist with daily tasks and activities.

- A support group.

- Knowledgeable professionals who they can call to ask questions and guidance if needed.

- Ways to set up a care-giver schedule with other family members if possible, so all of the care-giving doesn't fall upon one individual or family.

Chapter 2

GRACIOUS CARE-GIVING

Counseling and Serving with Sensitivity

Care-giving is Challenging, Important Work

Caring for a family member can be very difficult. In most instances the family member who is the primary care-giver is also the legal guardian or responsible party for the elderly individual. For the purposes of our discussion we will follow this same path.

Some older Americans have their care-giving needs met by a family member. Almost three-quarters of the disabled elderly receiving care-giver services depend entirely upon family or other unpaid help. An estimated 18 million family care-givers spend an average of ten hours a week assisting the elderly relative. About three-quarters of the care-givers are women, and most of them work outside the home. Many of them are raising children and some have grandchildren. They are wedged between the responsibilities of caring for both younger and older generations; they are over extended, stressed, guilt-plagued, and financially squeezed. They are a growing group who has been dubbed the "sandwich generation." They are the substance that is holding the older and younger generations.[38]

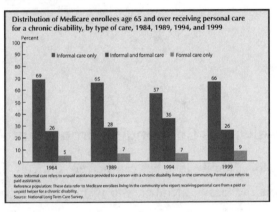

Distribution of Medicare enrollees age 65 and over receiving personal care for a chronic disability, by type of care, 1984, 1989, 1994, and 1999

Note: Informal care refers to unpaid assistance provided to a person with a chronic disability living in the community. Formal care refers to paid assistance.
Reference population: These data refer to Medicare enrollees living in the community who report receiving personal care from a paid or unpaid helper for a chronic disability.
Source: National Long Term Care Survey.

Before a major decision is made about becoming a primary care-giver, a person should set up a family meeting time. Concerns can be discussed and talked over with the immediate family household and then the remainder of the family. In these discussions, it is important to establish realistic goals, communicate with the whole family, and prioritize concerns so that there can be an appropriate balance in the many needs of family, work, and other commitments.

The idea of being a failure or success as a care-giver can only be determined by the individual care-giver. Each situation and set of circumstances is different. We all have our own definitions of success and can only do our best. As family members, care-givers, and Christian counselors we need to remind our clients that they cannot be guided by guilt, remarks, or opinions from others when they know that under the circumstances they did everything possible that could have been done at that time.

Finding the Right People for This Good Work

We all have 20/20 hindsight and can second guess decisions for many years. Undue stress and unnecessary guilt feelings are about the only true results that come from second guessing oneself. Each care-giver goes into this with different experiences, expectations, and life circumstances. We know that care-giving in the home is generally provided by one of two groups.

Professionally-Employed Care-Givers

Finding help is not always easy. It is better to look for services before we need them. The services that we request initially will change as our parent ages whether we are the primary care-giver or someone has been hired as a care-giver. What will need to be done before we hire a care-giver? Whether we hire an individual or an agency, there are some basic questions that we will want to ask before hiring anyone.

- Decide what tasks and activities that the care-giver will be expected to provide.

- Develop a job description so that everyone knows what the expectations are.

- Ask for references and call to check them out.

- Clearly explain expectations, and, if there are concerns, corrective explanations should be clear and specific.

- Find out what types of services they provide.

- Keep the lines of communication open.

- Provide basic information about the person receiving care. Even the most experienced care-giver needs to know the client's food likes and dislikes, medication schedule, daily schedule, and contact numbers.

Family Members or Friends as Care-Givers

Our society today is very mobile. About one in six Americans move each year. The median duration that people have lived in their current residence was 5.2 years. The average American moves 11.7 times in a lifetime.[39] In many instances family members become long distance care-givers because they are not able to move into the individual's residence or to the vicinity where the elderly individual lives due to employment, children, and financial limitations. A family member can be a long distance care-giver and still live in the vicinity. Generally what the long distance responsible party does is to hire a care-giver, or to ask a friend or neighbor to check in on the resident to see how they are doing and provide assistance as needed. The family member is still making all of the decisions except they are having a local care-giver inform them on how the elderly individual is progressing. The long distance care-giver will also visit the family member on the weekends or for a few days a month.

The other type of care-giver is when a family member moves into the senior's home or has the elderly individual move into the care-giver's residence. Care is now directed and assistance overseen by the family member.

Care-Givers and Burnout

Burnout is very prevalent when an individual becomes a care-giver—both volunteer and professional. Counselors and family members should consider this one of the first topics discussed when making care-giving choices. No one is immune to burnout and its effects. Almost everyone is prone to it—some more than others. It can sneak up on us without our even being aware that it has happened.

"Burnout" is a word used to describe a feeling of physical and emotional exhaustion which comes after we have had prolonged involvement with people and work situations that demand our time, energy, and strength. In the past, the term burnout was used in reference to an item not working any longer such as a light bulb or a small appliance. It was burned out, not usable anymore. But this can be prevented if the care-giver takes proper care of himself or herself.

Recently it has become apparent that counselors are not the only ones who experience burnout. Nurses, lawyers, pastors, physicians, sales people, business executives, and parents are among those who experience periodic burnout. In days gone by, the term burnout was used in reference to a defective light bulb or a game of catch, throwing the ball harder and harder and progressively faster each time until a player's hand was burning from the hard, fast throws.

Today, the meaning has to do with a mental and or physical condition of an individual. Burnout has become a catchall phrase by many people for situations and conditions that are in no way related to the burnout syndrome. It isn't easy for those in the people professions to interact intensely and continually with people who demand a lot from us, and are hurting or under pressure. Some of the people we live with and work with demand a lot of our time, energy, and concentration and are unable to give very much in return. In many instances we feel for and with them. If they hurt we hurt, if they are sad we are sad, and if they are pondering making a decision so are we. All of this can be a great strain for a person seeking to serve, to help, and to support another.

One of the most intensive studies on burnout was done at the University of California in Berkeley. Through their research they discovered that there are several signs which indicated that an individual was developing burnout. Some of the behavior indicators are:

- Detaching Self from Other People—Staying at home, spending less time with others, aloof, cynical, less involved emotionally.

- Beginning to Run Down Physically— Frequent headaches, fatigue, loss of physical energy, high blood pressure, cramps, sleepless- ness, arthritis, ulcers, and spasms.

- Influenced Psychologically—Low morale, forgetfulness, self-condemnation, and "what's the use?" attitude.

Many times when an individual starts experiencing burnout, he or she doesn't have the slightest idea what is going on. The temptation is to start trying to overcome problems by working harder. This only increases the frustration. In many instances the individual will take it out on family, and they will be the ones to suffer. Some sufferers will quit and change jobs and begin a repeat of the cycle again, and some will even get fired from their jobs. How do we break the cycle of burnout? How do we know if we are at risk for burnout?

Responses to Stress

The medical sciences have discovered that different types of personalities are predisposed to different medical problems under stress. The Type A (Melancholy, Choleric) personality is more prone to burnout than the Type B (Phlegmatic, Sanguine) personality. The Type A person is highly competitive, feels the pressure for time, and may react to frustration with hostility. The Type A person is more likely to set deadlines or quotas for themself at work or home at least once a week. The Type A person brings their work home frequently. This type of person is highly achievement oriented, and pushes himself to near capacity. Some behaviorists say that the Type A person earns the rewards they seek, but perhaps at the cost of their health. The Type A individual is at a greater risk for heart attack when under stress than the Type B individual. Along with the risk of heart attack there is also the possibility of migraines, tension headaches, asthma, colitis, backaches and an array of other physical maladies.[40]

The Type B personality puts in time at work and seldom brings work home. Interests tend to be more in sports and leisure time activities. This type is not a slave to time, and proving worth to self or others is not a strong personal requirement. The potential for intelligence is as strong as the Type A personality, but a Type B doesn't work at it. The Type B personality is less likely to demand strong control of life's circumstances or social environment. "Going with the flow" is the main goal. The tendency is to not fight the upstream battle like the salmon.

Whatever the personality type, coping, in many instances, isn't easy. We humans like to be able to control our own fate. One of the main things that increases stress is the feeling of loss of control. If we would accept the fact that we are not able to control all events we would be in a much better position to start managing stress. Stress is usually accompanied by feelings of arousal or agitation. When a person is undergoing stress he feels keyed-up and the problems become more evident when such arousals occur and actions become more primitive.

We can help each other—loved ones, counselors, caregiving clients, and fellow workers—avoid burnout. There are successful coping strategies that work, and we can overcome the situations and practice the strategies as needed. If an individual sees himself as passive and his future controlled by others, he is more susceptible to stress. If an individual has a self-concept of a more active nature, he is less susceptible to stress. If people could be persuaded to think of themselves in dynamic rather than static terms they might be more resistant to stress.

We need to get away from the labels that a situation is stressful because this creates a thinking pattern that the stress will go on forever. It is not as much the stress that is painful and disabling but our perception that it will never end. It will end, either in burnout or worse, if we do not cognitively take care of ourselves. According to the University of California in Berkeley study on burnout, some of the strategies that have proven successful are:

- The Need for Time Alone—Short rest breaks throughout the day or a few days vacation from the office, kids, and in-laws.

- Shared Responsibilities—Training subordinates to do the jobs we don't really need to do, and to remember that we cannot do it all, no matter what the television commercials say.

- Group Support—Networking with others in the same profession and other professions so that we can get their share of support and ideas.

- Proper Exercise and Diet—Can help in reduction of stress through toning up the body, relieving tension, getting energy, and maintaining strength through proper diet and exercise.

- Assertiveness—Knowing when we have too much to do. We can offer a polite *no* with a short statement that we are overbooked and could not give the project the proper attention that it needs at this time.

Burnout is a common experience among those in the people helping profession because they are expected to constantly and completely give to those in need. If burnout hasn't affected us, it has probably affected someone that we know. Burnout can be handled and conquered if we are aware of its influence and are willing to tackle it head on.

Another area that many care-givers think that they are immune to is elder abuse. As Christian counselors we should emphasize the importance of every care-giver or family member who is giving care to be sure that they:

- Are getting enough rest and relaxation so that they do not become angry, rough, ill-tempered, and slothful in providing care. As soon as we let these activities take hold we are pushing the line toward becoming an abusive care-giver.

- Are being observant that those providing care for your family member are being respectful and doing their job safely. Observe if there are bruises on the individual, loss of weight, or if the elderly individual's personality has changed.

- Are providing recreational and activity services through a third party the majority of the time. Research has shown that individuals who remain active often have higher levels of personal satisfaction in later life.

Summary of Later-Life Activity

The activities of older adults usually demonstrate the following characteristics:

- Most older individuals do not sit around with nothing to do. They have developed routines and activities over the years that usually fill their days and evenings.

- The individuals who are the most satisfied with their lives are usually engaged in regular activities outside the home that present challenges and relationships with friends and family.

- The activities do not usually occur in age-segregated settings.

- The activities that are the most significant are usually those that were satisfying in earlier years. The active old adult does select, replace, and start new activities. They enjoy and value these activities because they have established identities, competencies, self-images, values, and relationships.

- The activities that are most likely to attract older adults are built upon familiarity, established abilities, identities, interaction, and histories of satisfaction. What generally makes activity programs attractive is their quality, rather than any age designation.

- Activity programs that require older adults to redefine themselves as old, inferior, or incompetent are not going to be well attended, are not healthy, and should not be included. [41]

Both personal and social histories are important in the development of activity interest and abilities.

Filling time with events is not the objective. The objective is to provide enjoyable and familiar activities. Being entertained by others does not fulfill one's fundamental needs. Senior adults need activities that allow them to identify themselves as persons of worth and ability that are significantly related to others. There is nothing improper with modifying activities as needed. An individual might have played 18 holes of golf weekly but since the arthritis in the knees has worsened, he hasn't played golf in almost two years.

Some alternatives could be to develop a putting green in the yard or to take the individual to the golf course and practice hitting golf balls on the driving range. Another example of a modified activity might be for someone who has declining vision. If the individual enjoyed reading in the past and has difficulties seeing now, some modifications might be large print books, books on tape, Closed Caption TV (CCTV), magnifier, or talking devices. This will allow them to enjoy some of the past activities they had before their declining health.

It is imperative that we work judiciously in providing the most stress-free environment as possible. The benefits are innumerable when we are in the right environment. Depression is decreased or eliminated and health improves. The older adults develop positive attitudes. They become more motivated with a better overall look on life. Having said this, just a few adjustments, alterations, and modifications can make for a better relationship and quality of life for all involved.

Refer to the information below for a short test on stress. The Homes-Rahe Social Readjustment Rating Scale[42] can help determine if an individual is heading towards excessive stress or is already there.

The Holmes-Rahe Life Stress Inventory

Developed by Thomas Holmes and Richard Rahe. Homes-Rahe Social Readjustment Rating Scale, Journal of Psychosomatic Research. Vol. II, 1967.

How Stressed Are You?

The first step in reducing stress is becoming aware of the major sources of stress in your life. The following is a list of common stressors. Check all the boxes that apply. Your points will be totaled at the bottom of the test.

In the past 12 months, which of the following major life events have taken place in your life?

1. Make a check mark next to each event that you have experienced this year.

2. When you're done, add up the points for each event.

3. Check your score at the bottom.

_____ Death of spouse 100

_____ Divorce 73

_____ Marital separation 65

_____ Jail term 63

_____ Death of close family member 63

_____ Personal injury or illness 53

_____ Marriage 50

_____ Fired from work 47

_____ Marital reconciliation 45

_____ Retirement 45

_____ Change in family member's health 44

_____ Pregnancy 40

_____ Sex difficulties 39

_____ Addition to family 39

_____ Business readjustment 39

_____ Change in financial status 38

_____ Death of close friend 37

_____ Change to a different line of work 36

_____ Change in number of marital arguments 35

_____ Mortgage or loan over $10,000 31

_____ Foreclosure of mortgage or loan 30

_____ Change in work responsibilities 29

_____ Trouble with in-laws 29

_____ Outstanding personal achievement 28

_____ Spouse begins or stops work 26

_____ Starting or finishing school 26

_____ Change in living conditions 25

_____ Revision of personal habits 24

_____ Trouble with boss 23

_____ Change in work hours, conditions 20

_____ Change in residence 20

_____ Change in schools 20

_____ Change in recreational habits 19

_____ Change in church activities 19

_____ Change in social activities 18

_____ Mortgage or loan under $10,000 17

_____ Change in sleeping habits 16

_____ Change in number of family gatherings 15

_____ Change in eating habits 15

_____ Vacation 13

_____ Christmas season 12

_____ Minor violations of the law 11

_____ **Your Total Score**

Life Stress Scores

0-149   Low susceptibility to stress-related illness.

150-299   50 percent susceptibility to stress-related illness. Learn and practice relaxation and stress management skills and a healthy, well lifestyle.

300 and over   80 percent susceptibility to stress-related illness. Daily practice of relaxation skills is very important for your wellness. Take care of it now before a serious illness erupts or an affliction becomes worse.

This scale shows the kind of life pressure that you are facing. Depending on your coping skills or the lack thereof, this scale can predict the likelihood of your falling victim to a stress-related illness. The illness could be mild (like frequent tension headaches, acid indigestion, loss of sleep) or very serious illness (like ulcers, cancer, migraines).

Finding Daily Living Solutions— Step by Step

There are a significant number of tasks that will need to be completed. An emergency contact list is a very valuable and time-saving document to have.[43] A family care-giver will know most of the information that will be required to complete the emergency call contact list. This should be completed in advance and posted or made available for possible future use. This contact list will also allow others to make telephone calls when the primary care-giver is not available.

What are some of the duties that the counselee needs to immediately undertake since they have decided to take on the role and become the primary care-giver? Home safety is very important. As we age we do not heal, ambulate, or react as quickly as we did when we were younger. Depending upon why we are requiring care-giver assistance, we may have deficits in a couple of areas. We may have arthritis so we don't move as quickly. We may have early onset of dementia or Alzheimer's, which can cause us to be more forgetful or confused than in our younger days.

There is an enormous physical, psychological, and economic toll when an older person becomes injured. Falls among older people can be caused by hazards, both internal and external. Older women experience more falls than older men and these women are more likely to live alone. The frequency and severity of accidents in the home of older people emphasizes the need for modifications to the home to compensate for the declining physical functions of the individual. The most common accident sites in the home are the bathroom, kitchen, bedroom, and stairs. The most hazardous room in the house is the bedroom. This is where falls, fires, poisoning, and suffocation may occur.[44]

A thorough discussion with the elderly individual's physician should also be arranged before definitive choices and significant modifications are made to the residence. The physician can shed some light on the aging individual's health condition and what appropriate medical interventions may need to be taken. If you are unsure about a home modification and safety assessment, most hospitals or rehabilitation centers employ occupational or physical therapists who can complete a home assessment.

Facilitating Maximum Home Use and Safety

Modification to the home environment can be a key factor in increasing the likelihood of older persons remaining independent and injury-free in their homes and active in their communities as long as they desire.

What is a home modification? It is an adaptation to the living environment intended to increase ease of use, safety, security, and independence.

Some home modifications include:

- Lever door handles that operate easily with a push
- Handrails on both sides of staircase and outside steps
- Ramps for accessible entry and exit
- Walk-in shower
- Grab bars in the shower, by the toilet, and by the tub
- Hand-held, flexible shower head

- Lever-handed faucets that are easy to turn on and off
- Sliding shelves and lazy Susan in corner cabinet
- Easy grip C or D ring handles on cabinet doors and drawers

Home Modification can Promote Independence and Prevent Accidents

Many persons are living in older structures which are deteriorating to the point that they are hazardous and can contribute to falls and injuries. Home modification and repairs can help prevent accidents and falls. Research by the National Centers for Disease Control (CDC) suggests that one-third of home accidents can be prevented by modification and repair.

Home modifications can enhance comfort, increase safety, prevent injuries, and facilitate ongoing access to community social, recreational, and supportive activities and services.[45]

Removing barriers and safety hazards also helps reduce the stresses associated with the reduction in physical capabilities as people age. Following a home safety and modification checklist before the slightest change in the health of an older person is noticed can save a great deal of time and stress later on.[46]

Assistive Technology Terms and Concepts

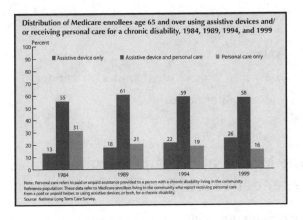

Distribution of Medicare enrollees age 65 and over using assistive devices and/or receiving personal care for a chronic disability, 1984, 1989, 1994, and 1999

Note: Personal care refers to paid or unpaid assistance provided to a person with a chronic disability living in the community. Reference population: These data refer to Medicare enrollees living in the community who report receiving personal care from a paid or unpaid helper, or using assistive devices, or both, for a chronic disability. Source: National Long Term Care Survey.

With assistive devices, many everyday tasks and chores can be completed safely, help prevent accidents, and promote independence. If an item compensates for functional limitations it is part of the broad category of assistive technology or assistive devices. Some devices can be very helpful even though they are not marketed as assistive technology. There are many factors that influence a person or should be considered before suggesting or introducing an assistive device. If the person doesn't understand the need for the device, feel it is needed, or want the item, they will probably not use it. We are required to use new things in our transactions and communications at such places as the bank, supermarket, and home. Because of constant changes there is the potential for older individuals to feel left out or alienated. We need to embrace technology and view it as a tool to improve our quality of life. The following devices are items that can be found relatively easily on the Internet or any medical supply store. These assistive devices can solve a multitude of problems and the user can be taught how to manipulate the devices in a relatively low time frame.

The Assistive Technologies listed in Chapter 3, **Grace-Filled Solutions**, offer solutions that can make daily living tasks easier to accomplish. These are only a representation of equipment available and address common problems older adults may experience.

Geriatric Care Manager

The care-giver who feels unqualified or unable to make decisions can hire a care manager. Generally a geriatric care manager is a nurse or social worker who is trained to work under difficult and trying circumstances. Their mission is to advocate for the care of the elderly individual by developing a care plan that considers the individual's health, quality of life issues, and financial status. A care manager will come and assess the individual and make recommendations concerning what type of help is needed, safety measures, and area agencies that supply services and equipment that are in the best interest of the parent. Before hiring a geriatric care manager or anyone else, you should ask for a reference and have a background check completed. If you are hiring a company to supply the geriatric care manager, ask for their references and whether they do background checks on their employees. Be cautious. Make sure you are comfortable with an individual or company and their skills before you hire them.

Cultural

The understanding of cultural factors is very vital to effective intervention with clients. Culture shapes attitudes and actions. It requires the understanding of roles and activities of older adults in a particular culture, attitudes about aging, and the way in which older individuals are valued by culture. These factors are mediated by:

- The sophistication of the culture.
- Changes in a culture over time.
- The degree to which the culture is settled in a specific place.
- Demographic factors such as the proportion of older versus younger individuals.[47]

There is a considerable difference between ethnic groups in the use of formal support services. Recent Vietnamese immigrants are less likely to use formal support services while recent Russian immigrants are more likely to use services. Mayerhoff theorizes that the reason for the use of services by elderly Russian immigrants is because they live a greater distance from their families and feel somewhat abandoned by them.[48]

Culture is the framework that guides and binds life practices. According to Anderson and Fenichel the, "… cultural framework must be viewed as a set of tendencies of possibilities from which to choose."[49] Cultural communities are made up of individuals, all of whom contribute their own unique characteristics to the sense of place in which they live. Differing cultures have different meanings or understandings of disabling and at-risk conditions. Each culture handles aging and disability situations in a different manner. The medical community needs to be trained to work closely with different cultures by becoming knowledgeable and aware of their values and family heritage. Some cultures live together generation after generation, and all in the same household. Other cultures encourage independence and the children leave the home when they become eighteen. This leaves the parents living alone in the household in their twilight years when they are most susceptible to needing help.

The older population will grow more diverse as the population grows. This reflects the demographic changes in the U.S. population as a whole over the last several decades. Programs and services for older Americans in 2050 will require greater flexibility to meet the needs of a more diverse population.

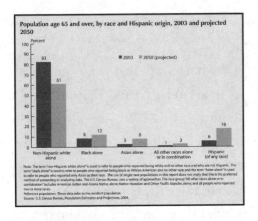

Population age 65 and over, by race and Hispanic origin, 2003 and projected 2050

In 2003, non-Hispanic whites accounted for nearly 83 percent of the older U.S. population. African-Americans make up just over 8 percent, Asians made up almost 3 percent and Hispanics (of any race) accounted for almost 6 percent of the older population. Estimates indicate that by 2050 the composition of the older population will be 61 percent non-Hispanic white, 18 percent Hispanic, 12 percent African-American and 8 percent Asian. The older population among all racial and ethnic groups is expected to grow. The older Hispanic population is projected to grow the fastest from just over 2 million in 2003 to 15 million in 2050 and be larger than the older African-American population by 2028. The older Asian population is also expected to increase. In 2003 nearly 1 million older Asians lived in the United States. And by 2050 this population is estimated to be almost 7 million. [50]

Personality Profiles

Family Dynamics

This is an area that is unique to each family. The goal and end result should always be the same: to do what is best for the individual needing care. Counseling individuals and family members concerning what the available options are and helping them to see the situation through Christ's eyes can be very difficult. Many times we will have a very good idea or know what the best solution is, but we might have a client who is not interested in what is best. The reason for this can be that the client has not been able to resolve their personal conflicts and until they do, they will not be able to receive the truth.[51] They might be wavering and stalling when a situation calls for an immediate answer. They might be choosing options that are contrary to all advice and best interest of those concerned. It is not always easy to understand why people do what they do or why they feel the way they do. Establishing caution may be one of the most difficult tasks facing a counselor. Some decisions—or lack of decisions—are made because of retaliation, anger, or guilt due to personality temperament. This is not always easy for the counselor to discern. But with prayer and the guidance of the Holy Spirit, he can know the truth.

Temperament and personality analysis can give us very accurate information as to how an individual will react in different situations. We can accurately predict the behavioral characteristics about how the older individual or family member(s) will react to most situations and circumstances. This is where a Christian counselor who is knowledgeable on senior issues can be a benefit. He can provide general information and guidance as to the process involved in elder care decisions. He will be able to explain some of the options and information to the individual, family members, and those involved to match their personality and how they interpret and digest information. Researchers over the years have studied temperament theory and categorized temperament theory into four basic temperament types: sanguine, melancholy, choleric, and phlegmatic. Knowing the personality types of those involved can give insight into how they will react to various circumstances and decisions that are made and will have to be made.

- Sanguine (strengths)—Talkative, outgoing, warm, enthusiasm, personable, friendly, compassionate, carefree.

- Sanguine (weaknesses)—Weak-willed, unstable, restless, undependable, egocentric, loud, exaggerates, fearful.

- Melancholy (strengths)—Gifted, analytical, sensitive, perfectionist, aesthetic, idealistic, loyal.

- Melancholy (weaknesses)—Self-centered, moody, negative, theoretical, impractical, unsociable, critical.

- Choleric (strengths)—Strong-willed, determined, independent, optimistic, practical, productive, leader.

- Choleric (weaknesses)—Crafty, unemotional, proud, angry-cruel, sarcastic, domineering, inconsiderate.

- Phlegmatic (strengths)—Calm, easy-going, dependable, efficient, conservative, diplomat, practical.

- Phlegmatic (weaknesses)—Stingy, fearful, indecisive, spectator, unmotivated, self-productive, selfish.[52]

Even though we are a mix and not simply one personality or the other, we can still come to a probable conclusion as to which temperaments will have a more difficult time of accepting an illness, declining health, or a change in living arrangements.

The Sanguine and Phlegmatic temperaments are more likely to accept a change in residence or serious illness. The Choleric and Melancholy individual would have a more difficult time adjusting to or accepting their situation and work hard to change it even if they knew it was unchangeable. When discussing personality theories it is important to remember that we are not one personality or the other, we are a blended personality. The blended personality is the mixing of personalities or temperaments cohesively together. Since we are usually more than one temperament, and if the strengths of each are used properly and the weaknesses de-magnified, the outcome desired can be positive. We cannot make a person over or redesign them. Everyone is slightly irregular and different from each other, even those with the same temperament classifications. This is a time to be uniting together with a focus on being Christ-like and "thinking His thoughts after Him."

Serving Graciously—Beyond Surface Emotions and Reactions to Aging

When individuals of different temperaments are working together effectively using their strengths and weaknesses as a team, they can produce the most positive outcomes possible.

We don't all need to be the same temperament to get along. We can blend together and be effective for the cause of Christ by remembering that we are all different temperament-wise, but serving the same risen Savior.

The Individual's Health Condition

The health of an individual will be as significant as their financial resources when an individual and his family are determining what the most appropriate living arrangement is. The living arrangement could be an assisted living center, home care, personal care home, or a nursing home. All of these housing options offer different levels of care, financial cost, and individual likes and dislikes. As we age and changes occur in our vision, cognition, mobility, hearing, and manual dexterity, assistive technology solutions are available.

Chronic diseases are long-term illnesses that rarely are cured. Some of the most common and costly chronic diseases include heart disease, stroke, cancer, and diabetes. Chronic health conditions affect the quality of life, negatively contributing to declines in functioning and the inability to remain in the home. Behavioral interventions could have prevented or modified many chronic illnesses. Of the leading causes of death among older Americans, 5 of the 6 leading causes are chronic diseases.[53]

Health and Housing Issues are Challenges to Be Faced with Grace

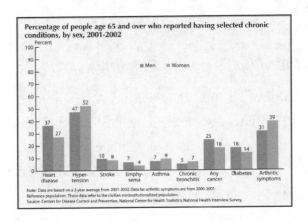

Percentage of people age 65 and over who reported having selected chronic conditions, by sex, 2001-2002

Note: Data are based on a 2-year average from 2001-2002. Data for arthritic symptoms are from 2000-2001. Reference population: These data refer to the civilian noninstitutionalized population. Source: Centers for Disease Control and Prevention, National Center for Health Statistics, National Health Interview Survey.

Occurrences of chronic conditions differ by sex. Statistics show that women report higher levels of hypertension, asthma, chronic bronchitis, and arthritic symptoms. Men reported higher incidences of heart disease, cancer, diabetes, and emphysema. There were also differences by race and ethnicity in the occurrence of certain chronic conditions. Among those sixty-five and over, non-Hispanic blacks reported higher levels of hypertension and diabetes than non-Hispanic whites—66 percent compared with 49 percent for hypertension and 23 percent compared with 14 percent for diabetes. Hispanics also report higher levels of diabetes than non-Hispanic whites—24 percent compared with 14 percent and both groups had similar levels of hypertension—48 percent. Some conditions have been showing an increase over time. About 47 percent of the people sixty-five and over reported having hypertension in 1997–1998 compared with 50 percent in 2001–2002. Diabetes is also increasing among the older population from 13 percent in 1997–1998 to 16 percent in 2001–2002.[54]

The respondent-assessed health ratings of good, very good, and excellent correlate with lower risk of mortality. The purpose for asking people to rate their health using one of the categories provides a common indicator of health, easily measured in surveys. It represents the physical, emotional, and social aspect of health and well-being.

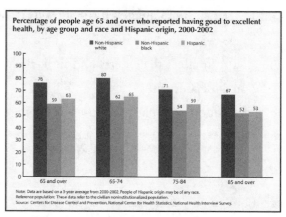

Older persons assessed their health as fair or poor—27 percent, compared to 9 percent for all populations in 2000. There was minimal difference between the sexes on this question. Older African-Americans—41.6 percent—and older Hispanics—35.1 percent—were more likely to rate their health as fair or poor than were older Whites—26 percent. The percentage of older Americans with disabilities increases significantly as age increases. Over 73.6 percent of those eighty and over reported at least one disability. Of these individuals 57.6 percent had one or more severe disabilities, and 34.9 percent required assistance due to a disability. The relationship between disability and health status is a vital predictor. Those sixty-five and older with a severe disability—68 percent—reported their health as fair or poor, and 10 percent of those who did not report a disability reported their health fair or poor. Lower income levels and lower educational attainment were associated in a greater degree with a severe disability. There are several conditions that can affect the elderly and limit their ability to live at home independently.[55]

Some of the conditions that can limit one's ability to live at home include:[56]

Arthritis

It affects about one in every six Americans. The two most common forms of arthritis are osteoarthritis and rheumatoid arthritis. Arthritis is a term that means joint inflammation and is a leading cause of disability in the United States. It typically makes the joints painful, stiff, and swollen, which can turn the simplest of everyday tasks into a painful ordeal that requires assistance to complete.[57]

Memory Impairment

Memory skills are important to general cognitive functioning. Declining scores on memory tests are one of several indicators that there is a cognitive loss of functioning. Low cognitive functioning such as memory impairment is a major health and safety risk factor to consider when contemplating which type of care-giving situation to implement. Depending upon the severity of the memory impairment, in home care is feasible, and in other circumstances moving the individual to a nursing home is the best option. Each set of choices and family circumstances are different, there is not a single answer or formula that works for everyone.

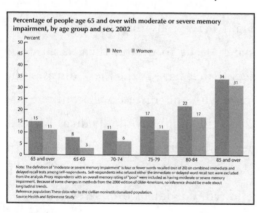

Percentage of people age 65 and over with moderate or severe memory impairment, by age group and sex, 2002

Older men are more likely to experience memory impairment of moderate to severe than older women. The percentage of men age sixty-five and over who experienced moderate to severe memory impairment was 15 percent compared with 11 percent for women. The differences narrowed at age eighty-five and over. Approximately one-third of both men and women experienced moderate to severe memory impairment. Moderate to severe memory impairment is six times as high for people age sixty-five and over. The proportion of people in 2002 over eighty-five years old and over with moderate or severe memory impairment was 32 percent compared with 5 percent for people whose age was sixty-five to sixty-nine.[58]

Alzheimer's is not the only disease that causes memory impairments or a decline in cognitive functioning, but it is the one that is the most recognized. Alzheimer's disease is not a normal part of aging. This disease affects the individual's brain nerve cells that impair memory, thinking, and ultimately leads to death. There is an estimated 4.5 million people that have Alzheimer's disease. The number of Americans with this disease will continue to grow. By the year 2050 the number of individuals with Alzheimer's is estimated to be between 11.3 million and 16 million. Age is the greatest risk factor and increases as an individual ages. One in ten individuals over sixty-five and nearly half of all those eighty-five and over are affected. A person with Alzheimer's disease will live an average of eight years from initial onset, however some live as many as twenty years from initial onset. The national direct and indirect costs of caring for individuals with Alzheimer's are estimated at 100 billion per year.[59]

Diabetes

The cause of diabetes is still unknown. This is a disease in which the body does not produce or properly use insulin. Insulin is a hormone that is needed to convert sugar, starches, and other food into energy needed for daily living. In the United States there are 18.2 million people who have diabetes and an estimated 5.2 million people who are unaware they have the disease.[60] Some of the conditions that can result from diabetes are impaired vision, stroke, slow healing or non-healing wounds, body weight issues, and neuropathy.

Sensory Impairments

The quality of life is limited for the elderly as their hearing, vision, and oral manipulation decreases. As the aging population increases over the next thirty years, the number of visual, hearing, and oral impairments will increase. They have more difficulties performing activities of daily living and communicating with others.[61] Older individuals are disproportionately affected by these losses. Vision and hearing impairments and oral health problems are often thought of as natural signs of aging. Early detection and treatment can prevent or postpone some of the debilitating physical, social, and emotional effects these impairments can have on the lives of older individuals. Under current Medicare guide-lines, glasses, hearing aids, and regular dental care are not covered services.[62]

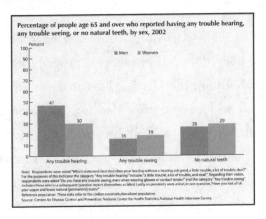

Percentage of people age 65 and over who reported having any trouble hearing, any trouble seeing, or no natural teeth, by sex, 2002

Close to one-half of the older men and one-third of the older women reported trouble hearing in 2002. The percentage of those who reported hearing difficulties was higher in the eighty-five and over at 60 percent compared to 30 percent for those sixty-five to seventy-four. 10 percent of all older women and 19 percent of all older men reported having ever worn a hearing aid.[63]

Location of Housing Option

It has been reported that more than 50,000 different housing options are now available for senior citizens. There are approx-imately 17,000 nursing homes and approximately 30,000 assisted living facilities in the United States. The availability and location is dictated by market demand in most instances.

Currently more than 22 million households provide some type of care for a family member, friend, or loved one.[64]

In the larger cities there are more choices and services to choose from when looking for some type of assistance. That doesn't always translate into availability or acceptable care. Also, depending upon the time of year, the vacancies can vary significantly. During the holiday season and summer there are generally more resident room openings. This can be attributed to more family members being available to help take on the role of care-giver. Some older people living in the community have access to additional services through their place of residence. These services may include meal preparation, laundry, cleaning services, and assistance with medications. These services are designed through the place of residence to help them maintain their independence and avoid transferring to another location where services are directed at those individuals who are less able to care for themselves.

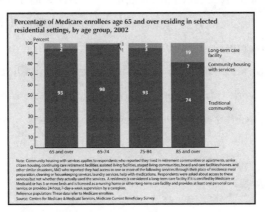

The living arrangements of the older population are important indicators because they are linked to income, health status, and the availability of care-givers. Older Americans who live alone are more prone to live in poverty than are the older people who live with their spouses.

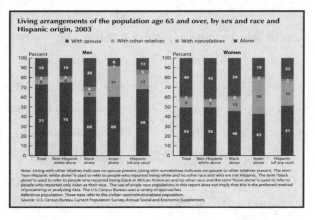

Older women were more likely to live alone than older men. In 2003 about 50 percent of the women and 73 percent of the men lived with their spouses. Twice as many older women (40 percent) were as likely to live alone compared to 19 percent of the men. The living arrangements of older people differed by race and Hispanic origin. Older Asian women were more likely to live with relatives other than a spouse. Older non-Hispanic white and black women (40 percent) were more likely than others to live alone.

Financial Resources

It has been stated that older Americans live in adequate affordable housing but some older Americans now have to budget a larger portion of their financial resources toward housing.

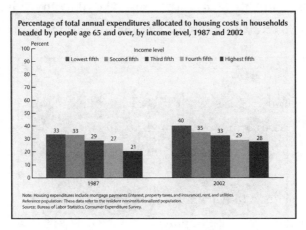

Percentage of total annual expenditures allocated to housing costs in households headed by people age 65 and over, by income level, 1987 and 2002

When housing expenses comprise a relatively high proportion of total expenses there is less money available for health care, saving, and other important goods and services. Since the costly burden of housing is relative to expenditures, these other expenditures decline as income increases. Those sixty-five and over in 2002 whose income was in the bottom fifth of income distribution allocated an average of 40 percent of all basic expenditures to basic housing.[65]

The proportions declined to about 33 percent for those in the middle income fifth percent and to 28 percent for those in the top fifth of the income distribution. The households in the lowest income group in 2002 spent $5,116 compared to $11,544 spent on housing by those in the highest income group.[66] Older Americans are retired from full-time work. When Social Security was initially introduced it was designed to supplement an individual's pension and other income from assets. Currently Social Security has taken on a greater importance and is the major source of income for many Americans.[67]

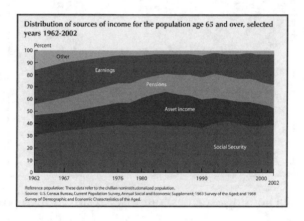

Distribution of sources of income for the population age 65 and over, selected years 1962-2002

Governmental Assistance for Aging Americans

Social Security has provided the largest share of income for older Americans since the 1960s. The share from all other income resources pensions and earnings has risen slightly over the last 10 years while income from assets has declined. "A MetLife Mature Market Institute poll found that a majority of the Baby Boomers believe they are not going to need ongoing health care during their retirement years." They think they will have no need for making financial provisions for long-term care, according to the survey. Seventy-nine percent have little or no concern regarding having enough money to live in their retirement years comfortably. Sixty-two percent planned to use Medicare to pay for long-term care services. Another forty percent expect to use health insurance—a misconception about what funding sources are available for this type of care. "This study shows us that Americans need to be better informed about their retirement living and long-term care options in retirement so that they can make the right decisions about their needs."[68]

Medicare Program

The Medicare program is a health insurance for the disabled and aged. The program is administered by the Center for Medicare and Medicaid Services. Medicare Part A is provided free to those who qualify and receive Social Security payments. The program consists of two parts, A and B. Part A provides coverage for the cost by eligible beneficiaries for inpatient hospital care, inpatient care in a nursing facility following a hospital stay, home health care, and hospice services. Each of the services has specific conditions that must be met before Medicare services are provided.[69] Part B is a voluntary program that eligible beneficiaries who pay a monthly premium are entitled to have physicians and other medical service providers reimbursed. Medicare will not pay for care that is primarily custodial.

Medicaid Program

The Medicaid program is administered by each individual state and is designed for the disabled and low income. Each state has specific requirements for acceptance into the program. The maximum financial amount allowed varies from state to state. If you have questions concerning Medicaid and eligibility, it is best to contact a Medicaid office or an expert who specializes in these types of benefits. If a patient is married, he can expect the income from individuals and their combined assets will be considered in determining Medicaid eligibility to support the remaining spouse at home. Generally a person is required to use a significant portion of their assets to meet their expenses before payment proceeds.

Medical Care Options

Predicting what type of treatments patients will want at the end of life is complicated by:

- The individual's age.
- The nature of the illness.
- The ability of medical science and pharmacology to sustain life.
- The emotions of the family, patient request, and medical diagnosis outcomes.[70]

This is compounded by the gathered facts from the U.S. Department of Census:

- Less than 50 percent of the severely or terminally ill had an advance directive.
- Over 70 percent of physicians whose patients had advance directives were not aware that it existed.
- Surrogates named in the advance directives often were not present to make decisions or were too emotionally overwrought to offer guidance.

Advance Planning—A Graceful and Practical Part of Aging

Advance planning is a way to protect the whole family and let everyone know what you have decided. This avoids questioning, second-guessing, and fighting. Individuals with chronic diseases go through periods of slowly declining health marked by severe episodes that require hospitalization. This sequence can be repeated a number of times as person's health declines until they eventually expire. A legal document also known as a medical directive or advance directive can assist in eliminating a significant amount of confusion, guilt, and arguing among family members. These documents declare your wishes regarding life-supports or other medical treatment in specific medical circumstances. Advance directives are written documents, which formally states personal preferences for how medical decisions will be made if a person loses the ability to make them for himself. Living Wills are a legal document also known as a medical directive or advance directive. It states a person's wishes regarding life support or other medical treatment in certain circumstances, usually when death is imminent. A durable power of attorney is a legal document that enables an individual to designate someone else, called the attorney-in-fact, to act on his or her behalf in the event the document's author becomes disabled or incapacitated. Life is sacred and each individual should have their wishes documented well in advance concerning end-of-life decisions.

Caring Connections has advance directives, Living Will forms and durable power of attorney forms for all 50 states. You can find these forms and more at www.caringinfo.org. The forms are state specific because of the variations in the law from state to state. These forms can be found on other web sites, or an attorney could also compile the information for these types of documents. For educational purposes the appendix has a sample of a living will, durable power of attorney, advance directives, and the instructions for completing them.[71] As Christian counselors we should recommend to our clients that they have the proper documentation completed and filed with the appropriate agencies. Individuals should also keep a copy of documents for future references. If there are any questions concerning the documentation and what the proper meaning is, each counselee should discuss their questions with a medical professional and an attorney so there are not any mixed messages or assumptions by those concerned.

Health Care Provider Availability

Services will continue to be available but will change as health care changes. More and more Baby Boomers are planning on staying home during their golden years as long as possible. Some seniors are moving into housing communities that offer health and wellness programs. There is a shortage of medical personnel that is predicted to grow as the number of Baby Boomers increases. This could have a negative impact on the type of medical services offered. The negative impact would be less direct care by physicians, higher medical cost, increased home health, over-the-counter purchases, and natural remedies.

Many times the choice that an individual makes concerning senior housing options has to be made immediately. Often with limited resources and knowledge concerning available choices, a decision must be made. As we progress there will be few adult children and family members whose lives will not be touched directly or indirectly by an aging loved one who needs some measure of care. According to a Metropolitan Life Insurance Company study, the number of centurions would have reached 100,000 by the year 2000, and by 2050 the number could reach a total of 850,000–1 million 100-year-old men and women. The older population—sixty-five and older—numbered 35 million in 2000, an increase of 3.7 million from 1990 (U.S. Bureau of the Census). The number of Americans aged forty-five to sixty-four who will reach 65 over the next two decades will increase by 34 percent during this decade (U.S. Bureau of the Census). About one in every eight or 12.4 percent of the population is an older American. Over 5,574 persons celebrated their sixty-fifth birthday per day in 2000.[72] Members of minority groups are projected to represent 25 percent of the older population in 2030, up 16 percent in 2000 (U.S. Bureau of the Census, 2000).[73] Our society is aging and living longer thanks to the fields of nutrition, science, and medicine. Our life expectancy has reached a new high according to the U.S. Department of Health & Human Services in their 2002 report.

A significant number of alternative living arrangements is available for an individual who is unable to safely live at home alone. Each living arrangement is designed to provide a specific level of care and services depending upon the established admittance criteria. The alternative living market is continually evolving as the adult population ages. As the market expands, there are an increasing number of names that are used to describe living options. Many of these names are regional and in some instances either outdated terminology or new and evolving descriptive terms used to address the changes in society.

Housing Options—Alternative Living Arrangements

Joint Living with Adult Children

This type of living arrangement is when the parent moves into the home of the child/care-giver. This type of arrangement is also the one that generally has the least amount of success because the decision is based on emotion, not fact. Before this type of living arrangement is considered, all possible scenarios should be considered:

- What do the other family members in the home think of this type of arrangement?
- Is the dwelling large enough and what personal possessions will they want to bring?
- Is the home safe and free of obstacles?
- Can they be left home alone or do they need constant supervision?
- Does your lifestyle allow for you to be at home more?

- Can you release your privacy?
- Do your personalities mesh or conflict with each other and other members in the house?

Staying Home by Scaling Down

This is when a relatively healthy and independent senior citizen moves into a smaller residence because they can no longer care for a larger residence.

Elder Cottage Housing Opportunity—ECHO

This is the placing of a pre-build self-contained cottage also known as "granny flats" in the back or side yard of a single-family house. This type of arrangement allows for the parents to live next to their children while both households are able to retain most of their privacy. These housing units include barrier-free features and can be designed to fit the current building structure design, style, and color. Some units can be rented, installed, and removed when no longer needed. This concept is credited with originating in Australia.[74]

Home Sharing

The idea of home sharing is when someone other than a child moves into the home or apartment. The arrangements and caregiving duties depend on what the individuals have agreed upon. In some instances the individual moving in agrees to help with particular lists of caregiving tasks in exchange for free rent, partial rent, or paycheck and rent for care-giver services rendered.

Accessory Apartment

In this variation on home sharing, the parent's home is remodeled to include a self-contained apartment with a separate entrance. The apartment can be rented out to gain income or services can be rendered in exchange for free or reduced rent.

Adult Foster Care

This type of housing is generally for those who are frail but in reasonably good health. Adult foster homes provide lodging, meals, supervision, and no medical personal care. Most homes are privately owned and have one to twenty residents, depending upon the size of the home and state regulations.

Congregate Housing

This type of housing definition includes retirement hotels and retirement apartments. These services vary depending on price, location, and state. Generally one or more meals are offered daily. Housekeeping, recreation, transportation, and security are also offered on a limited basis.

Retirement Communities

Included in this type of housing is apartments, mobile homes, town homes, condominiums, and cooperatives developed especially for senior citizens who are relatively capable of safely living alone.

Assisted Living Facilities

This is a relatively new type of housing and is also known as personal care homes, residential care facilities, or sheltered care and adult care homes. These are places for older adults who need some assistance with daily living activities but who do not require skilled nursing care.

Continuing Care Retirement Communities – CCRC

Continuing care retirement communities offer varying levels of care. They start with not requiring assistance and progress to levels that provide some assistance with daily living activities. The independent level is where the individual can live alone safely. Whenever there is a level decline in independence the resident is moved to a residence area where more care is required.

Nursing Homes

This is a facility where twenty-four hour health care and services are provided. This type of facility has the worst stigma and psychological attachments to the old folk's home, retirement home, skilled nursing facility, and the name nursing home due to the pure nature of their business—caring for the elderly who are sick, disabled, and nearing the end of their life expectancy. The poor services and care of a small percentage of nursing homes has caused a negative view of this type of living facility.

There are options available to assist the care-giver when he is looking to find an alternative living arrangement but what are they, where are they, and can they assist him? It is very stressful to make the decision that a family member cannot live at home alone safely. But having to find alternate living arrangements can be even more stressful. In most instances the family will need to quickly decide upon alternate housing arrangements because the family member has become ill or had an accident. When this happens the care-giver is not usually able to care for them anymore and a social worker or physician is recommending that they move to some type of care facility where there is twenty-four hour care available.

Most individuals do not know where to look, what to look for, or questions to ask the care facility. This is where the Christian counselor can be a tremendous resource. Knowing where to look for a care facility and what questions to ask can relieve a family of a tremendous burden. The care-giver can locate information through various local or national organizations, churches, hospitals, libraries, publications, web sites, and brochures.

Resources for Considering Assisted Living Options

The guides and checklists on the following pages are designed to be used as evaluative and decision-making resources. The Senior Housing Guide is designed to try and get answers to some of the frequently asked questions during a visit. The Care Facility Profile form is designed to make telephone inquires before the visit so that a list of possible choices can be narrowed down especially when time is limited. It is very beneficial when the telephone screening form is used if someone else can assist so that information can be compared and a decision can be made as to which care facilities warrant a visit.

Appendix D lists resources for additional research on Housing Options and Organizations. Recommended Reading and Health Information web sites are also cited.

SENIOR HOUSING GUIDE CHECKLIST
ON SITE VISITATION CHECKLIST

Name of Senior Home: _____

Visit Date: _____

Basic Information

❑   The senior home is Medicare-certified.

❑   The senior home is Medicaid-certified.

❑   The senior home has the level of care needed (e.g., skilled, custodial), and a bed is available.

❑   The senior home has special services if needed in a separate unit (e.g., dementia, ventilator, or rehabilitation), and a bed is available.

❑   The senior home is located close enough for friends and family to visit.

Residents Appearance

❑   Residents are clean, appropriately dressed for the season or time of day, and well groomed.

Senior Home Living Spaces

❑   The senior home is free from overwhelming unpleasant odors.

- ❏ The senior home appears clean and well kept.
- ❏ The temperature in the senior home is comfortable for residents.
- ❏ The senior home has good lighting. Noise levels in the dining room and other common areas are comfortable.
- ❏ Smoking is not allowed, or may be restricted to certain areas of the senior home.
- ❏ Furnishings are sturdy, yet comfortable and attractive.

Staff

- ❏ The relationship between the staff and the residents appears to be warm, polite, and respectful.
- ❏ All the staff wears name tags. Staff knocks on the door before entering a resident's room and refer to residents by name.
- ❏ The senior home offers a training and continuing education program for all staff.
- ❏ The senior home does background checks on all staff.
- ❏ The guide on your tour knows the residents by name and is recognized by them.
- ❏ There is a full-time Registered Nurse (RN) in the nursing home at the senior home at all times, other than the Administrator or Director of Nursing.

❏ The same team of nurses and Certified Nursing Assistants (CNAs) work with the same resident four to five days per week.

❏ CNAs work with a reasonable number of residents.

❏ CNAs are involved in care planning meetings.

❏ There is a full-time social worker on staff.

❏ There is a licensed doctor on staff. Is he or she there daily? Can he or she be reached at all times?

❏ The senior home's management team has worked together for at least one year.

Residents' Rooms

❏ Residents may have personal belongings and/or furniture in their rooms.

❏ Each resident has storage space (closet and drawers) in his or her room. Each resident has a window in his or her bedroom.

❏ Residents have access to a personal telephone and television.

❏ Residents have a choice of roommates.

❏ Residents can reach water pitchers.

❏ There are policies and procedures to protect residents' possessions.

❏ Hallways, stairs, lounges, and bathrooms exits are clearly marked.

❏ There are quiet areas where residents can visit with friends and family.

❏ The senior home has smoke detectors and sprinklers.

❏ All common areas, resident rooms, and doorways are designed for wheelchair use.

❏ There are handrails in the hallways and grab bars in the bathrooms.

Menus and Food

❏ Residents have a choice of food items at each meal. Are residents' favorite foods served?

❏ Nutritious snacks are available upon request.

❏ Staff helps residents eat and drink at mealtimes if help is needed.

Activities

❏ Residents, including those who are unable to leave their rooms, may choose to take part in a variety of activities.

❏ The senior home has outdoor areas for resident use and staff helps residents go outside.

❏ The senior home has an active volunteer program.

Safety and Care

❑	The senior home has an emergency evacuation plan and holds regular fire drills.

❑	Residents get preventive care, like a yearly flu shot, to help keep them healthy.

❑	Residents may still see their personal doctors.

❑	The senior home has an arrangement with a nearby hospital for emergencies.

❑	Care plan meetings are held at times that are convenient for residents and family members to attend whenever possible.

❑	The senior home has corrected all deficiencies (failure to meet one or more Federal or State requirements) on the previous state inspection report.

Additional Comments

_____

_____

_____

CARE FACILITY PROFILE

Initial telephone interview or mail to care facility to complete and return.

Care Facility:

- ❏ Care Facility Name: _____
- ❏ Address: _____
- ❏ City: _____ Zip Code: _____
- ❏ County: _____
- ❏ Phone: (   )_____

  Fax: (   )_____
- ❏ E-Mail: _____

Care Facility Staff:

- ❏ Administrator: _____
- ❏ Assistant Administrator: _____
- ❏ Admissions Coordinator: _____
- ❏ Director of Nursing: _____

Payment Types Accepted (please check all that apply):

- ❏ Medicaid
- ❏ Medicare
- ❏ Private Pay
- ❏ Veterans
- ❏ Private Insurance

Health Services Offered (please check all that apply):

- ❏ Skilled Nursing Care
- ❏ Alzheimer/Dementia Care Unit
- ❏ Private Pay Rooms
- ❏ Incontinence Program
- ❏ Pain Management Program
- ❏ Physical Therapy
- ❏ Occupational Therapy
- ❏ Speech/Language Therapy
- ❏ Stroke Rehabilitation Program
- ❏ Wound Care
- ❏ Podiatry Services
- ❏ Recreational Therapy
- ❏ Medical Director
- ❏ 24-Hour Nursing Care
- ❏ Hospice Services
- ❏ Sub-Acute Unit
- ❏ Pharmacy
- ❏ Respiratory Therapy
- ❏ Dietitian

Care Facility Services/Features

(please check all that apply):

- ❏ Dining Room
- ❏ Day Room

- ❏ TV Room
- ❏ Beauty / Barber Shop
- ❏ Library
- ❏ Worship Services
- ❏ Laundry Services
- ❏ Outdoor/Patio Area
- ❏ Activities Room
- ❏ Room Visitations
- ❏ Special Activities
- ❏ Movies
- ❏ Activities / Games
- ❏ Crafts
- ❏ Intergenerational Programs
- ❏ Exercise Group
- ❏ Holiday Activities

Mission/Purpose

_____

_____

_____

_____

_____

_____

_____

Optional—Narrative:

Please list all those features, services or activities that make this facility **"Special."**

_____

_____

_____

_____

_____

_____

_____

The Graying of America

As the elderly population grows, families will need assistance in locating suitable care facilities **and to find necessary resources.** Statistics show that 4 out of every 10 people turning 65 will have the need for part or full-time nursing care at some point in their lives.[75] As our population ages, the demand for these services will only continue to grow. There is help for finding acceptable care facilities within a convenient distance for needed families.

In 1999, Baby Boomers represented almost 30 percent of the U.S. population. Over the next twelve to thirty years, they'll age to sixty-five and older. That means that by 2030, one in every five Americans will be at least sixty-five years of age.[76]

Living Longer

That statistic, combined with the longevity in this country, greatly magnifies the importance of finding quality resources and optional services. The age group of eighty-five and older is the fastest-growing segment of the American population today. In fact, the number of people belonging to this group has more than tripled since 1970.[77] As more of us are living into these later years, we're more likely to experience chronic illnesses, disabilities, and dependency. In locating, recognizing, and compiling the quality resources, it will be possible to alleviate some of the complications involved in finding a variety of resource choices for the individual.

Growing Old with Grace

The Lord has provided Christian counselors and other caregivers with wonderful opportunities to spread His Word boldly to those we serve. God's amazing grace to us includes His provision of services and programs to assist the elderly and their loved ones when age and health issues make it impractical for the aged to live safely at home alone.

What can be done to help? There is a need for Christian counselors who want to work in this area of specialization. This specialization can be very intense, time consuming, and will require a significant amount of time outside of the normal counseling program to become effective and competent. In addition to the regular counseling program, a counselor should be resourceful and versed in such areas as research, health issues, physiology, assistive technology, Medicare, and home modifications.

Because of the amount of time, effort, and energy involved, senior issues/elderly counseling is not for everyone. It is my belief that those who enter into this area should have a leading of the Holy Spirit. As America grays and the elderly population grows at a phenomenal rate over the next twenty years, there will be a need for Christian counselors who are trained in and understand aging issues.

Chapter 3

GRACE-FILLED SOLUTIONS

Practical Information to Assist the Aging with Resources for Daily Living

Practical Information

"What can I do?" That is a common question many individuals ask as they start the role of primary care-giver or are assisting in the care giving role. It's important to remember that safety and keeping the home free from potential hazards are of the utmost importance. "How do I make the home safer?" "How can I make things easier for them?" Whether the individual needing assistance lives at home alone or lives with someone else, modifications will still probably need to be made. The following information is not all inclusive due to varying housing environments, but can be useful in helping set up a safer, friendly environment. The Emergency Call Contact List[78] contains a place for the names and numbers an individual might need in case of an emergency. The Emergency Contact List should be kept in a visible, easy-to-reach location, such as by the telephone(s) or on the side of the refrigerator. The Home Safety Modification Checklist can be completed with minimal expense and relative ease. The checklist walks you through each room in the house with modification suggestions to consider making so that the living environment might be safer.

EMERGENCY CALL CONTACT LIST
In Case Of An Emergency: Call 911

Family Members To Contact in a Emergency

Name: _____

Telephone Number: _____

Name: _____

Telephone Number: _____

Name: _____

Telephone Number: _____

Name: _____

Telephone Number: _____

Name: _____

Telephone Number: _____

Physicians

Name: _____

Medical specialty: _____

Telephone Number: _____

Name: _____

Medical specialty: _____

Telephone Number: _____

Name: _____

Medical specialty: _____

Telephone Number: _____

Dentist

Name: _____

Medical specialty: _____

Telephone Number: _____

Pharmacy

Name: _____

Telephone Number: _____

Friends and Neighbors

Name: _____

Telephone Number: _____

Name: _____

Telephone Number: _____

Name: _____

Telephone Number: _____

Name: _____

Telephone Number: _____

HOME SAFETY & MODIFICATION CHECKLIST

Security

❑ Post important numbers in an easy to read format beside all telephones.

❑ Check to determine if all window and door locks are operable.

❑ If the family member wanders outside the home, install chain locks out of reach.

❑ Consider a commercially monitored emergency alert system if the elderly family member lives at home alone the majority of the time.

❑ Be sure to have extra keys and combinations of all locks for emergency purposes. If possible give a set of keys to a near by trusted friend who can also help out in an emergency.

Around the House

❑ Pick up all throw rugs, scatter rugs, or mats so they do not cause an accident by slipping on or tripping over.

❑ Be sure that all fixtures have the proper size lightbulb and are in working condition.

❑ Check the furnace to be sure it is working properly and clean out the filters.

- ❏ Regularly check all fire alarms to be sure they are in working condition.
- ❏ Keep extra batteries for the most commonly used items.
- ❏ Lower the hot water to 120 degrees or lower to prevent burns.
- ❏ Rearrange furniture for larger areas and more space to move around.
- ❏ If holding, turning, or grabbing doorknobs is difficult, change door handles to long-handled levers.
- ❏ Repair uneven and broken concrete steps, sidewalks, and other walking areas.
- ❏ Install railings by outdoor steps.
- ❏ Keep steps, sidewalks, and other walking areas free from leaves, snow, and ice.
- ❏ Lock basement doors.
- ❏ Consider an alarm to let a resident know when a door has been opened.

Bathroom

- ❏ Place nonskid strips in all tubs and showers.
- ❏ Place a nonskid bath mat next to shower and tub.
- ❏ Install grab bars around/in the bathtub/shower and by the toilet to assist in standing.
- ❏ Check that all towel bars are secured tightly.

❑ Be sure there are not any electrical appliances in the bathroom.

❑ A raised toilet seat may help if the individual has difficulties getting up.

❑ Be sure all faucets are well marked.

❑ If holding, turning, or grabbing items is difficult change faucet handles to long-handled faucet levers.

Kitchen

❑ Remove stove and oven knobs if the elderly individual is confused or cognitively impaired. Store these items out of reach so they do not turn on these appliances and injure themselves.

❑ Put the most commonly used kitchen items in an easy-to-reach location. Having to reach up too high or bend too low to get kitchen items can also initiate an accident or injury.

❑ Keep electrical appliances away from the sink.

❑ Store sharp knives and utensils in a safe location.

❑ Remove step stools.

❑ Keep towels and flammable items away from the stove.

❑ Put a fire extinguisher in the kitchen.

Bedrooms

- ❑ Keep a flashlight, telephone, and lamp at the bedside for easy reach.
- ❑ Consider installing handrails in the hallway and between the bedroom and bathroom if ambulation is unsteady.

Stairs and Hallways

- ❑ If climbing stairs is too difficult, consider relocating the individual's bedroom to the main floor. A stair glide is also an option that can assist the elderly with going up and down the steps.
- ❑ Keep stairs and hallways free of clutter.
- ❑ Install handrails the complete length of the stairway.
- ❑ Install nonskid strips on uncarpeted areas.
- ❑ Remove all step and floor covering that is ripped or in poor condition.

Assistive Living Technology Devices Guide

Universal Design

"Changes in who we are and what we can do require a world that is more accommodating to variances in mobility, vision, hearing, cognition, and manual dexterity. Universal design is an approach to creating everyday environments and products that are usable by all people to the greatest extent, regardless of age or ability; just as the modifying of an environment within a home makes it more accessible for increased independence."[79] Some universal design features include stepless houses, door levers, wider doorways, raised electrical outlets, inferred devices, and wider walk-in showers.

Assistive Technology

As defined by the Technology-Related Assistance for Individuals with Disabilities Act of 1988, an assistive device is an item or product (whether homemade, acquired commercially, modified, or customized) that is used to increase, maintain, or improve functional capacities of an individual. It may be handled, carried, or in some other way be in direct contact with the person. The assistive device may be placed in or attached to the environment or used within it to compensate for or alleviate a potential problem. Assistive devices can be very beneficial for the older individual because of age-related changes and accompanying diseases often resulting in functional impairments that lead to a reduction in or loss of independence.[80] Assistive devices help us overcome obstacles even when there has been a decline in physical function.

The products that appear below are provided by Maxi-Aids Inc. They are available at www.maxiaids.com, 1-800-522-6294, or 42 Executive Blvd., Farmingdale, NY 11735.

Maxi-Aids will gladly provide free catalogs that contain over 244 pages filled with helpful items, simply by using any of the contact methods above.

Vision Enhancers

Low Vision: Eyeglasses, large print playing cards, screen magnifier for computer or TV, large button telephone, bright colored objects.

Blind: Braille books, books on tape, guide cane, screen reader for computer, electronic book reader.

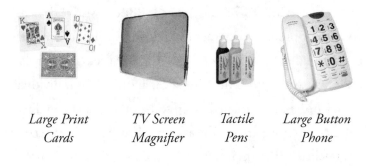

| *Large Print Cards* | *TV Screen Magnifier* | *Tactile Pens* | *Large Button Phone* |

Living Room

Difficulty getting in/out of a soft low chair: Board under cushion, automatic seat lift, pillow or blanket to raise seat, swivel and rocking chairs with device to lock motion.

Accessing, reaching, and seeing light switches: Touch-sensitive switches, voice-activated light switches, illuminated wall plates.

Position Lift Chair   *Seat Assist*   *Door Lever Extender*   *Lamp Switch Turner*

Bedroom

Bed too Low or unstable: Leg extensions, blocks, additional mattress, remove wheels, block against bed.

Difficulty getting in/out of bed: Portable bed rail, bed pole.

Difficulty hearing clock: Clock with light and vibration attachment.

Difficulty seeing clock: Large-faced clock, talking talk.

Distance from bathroom: Bedside commode, urinal.

Access to clothes: Place clothes in easy-to-reach drawers, shelves, or hangers.

Nighttime callers: Bedside phone, cordless phone, intercom.

Talking Alarm Clock   *Bed Rail*   *Large Clock w/Vibrator*   *Bedside Commode*

Bathroom

Getting on/off toilet: Raised seat, side safety bars, grab bars.

Getting in/out of tub: Grab bars, bath/stool chair, transfer bench, hand-held shower, hydraulic lift bath seat.

Slippery or wet floors: Non-skid rugs or mats.

Shower Stool   Safety Bars   Non-Skid
Shower/ Mat

Handheld   Long Handle Rotating
Shower   Seat Bath Sponge

Kitchen

Difficulty opening containers: Electric jar opener, electric can opener, multi-purpose opener.

Difficulty holding or keeping items stable: Large handle items, non-slip mats and strips, double handle cups, cutting board with suction cups and food stabilizer, pot stabilizer.

Difficulty seeing measurements and time: Auto-measure device, large number timer, talking thermometer.

Difficulties cutting and chopping food: Electric chopper, vegetable/fruit slicer, rocker knife, cut resistant gloves.

| *Multi-Purpose 4 Way Opener* | *Easy Grip Mug* | *Select A Spice Measure Auto Carousel* | *Two-Handled Mincing Rocker Knife* |

Telephone

Difficulty reaching: Cordless phone, inform friends to let ring longer, answering machine.

Difficulty hearing ring: Ring amplifier, blinking or flashing lights, vibrating ringer.

Difficulty holding receiver: Headset, speakerphone, adapted handles.

Difficulty hearing other people: Amplified volume control, text telephone (TTY, TDD), headset, hearing aid compatible.

Difficulty dialing numbers: Pre-set memory dial, large buttons and numbers, voice activated dialing, all phones synchronized with the same preset memory numbers, picture phone.

*Voice-Activated
Dialer Telephone*

TTY

*Large Button
Phone*

*Phone Alert
Flasher*

Photo Dial

Medication

Difficulty opening: Use pill cap opener, have dispensers filled by pharmacist, blister packs.

Difficulty reading labels: Use magnifying glass, large print, good lighting.

Difficulty remembering medication schedule: Medication organizer, automatic pill dispenser, medication call reminder.

| *Magnifying Medicine Cap Remover* | *Weekly Medication Keeper* | *Daily Medication Manager* | *Talking Monthly Medication Organizer and Alarm* |

General Safety

Difficulty locking doors: Remote controlled door lock, combination door lock, door wedge.

Difficulty reaching: Long handle reacher, push/pull stick, long shoehorn.

Difficulty opening door or knowing who is there: Automatic door openers, intercom at door, lever doorknob handles, video intercom.

Can't hear alarms: Smoke detectors, phone ringing or doorbell: blinking lights, vibrating surfaces.

Smoke Detector Kit with Vibrator and Strobe   *Indoor/Outdoor Motion Detector*   *Extendable Flashlight with Magnet*   *Blinking Door Alert*

Leisure

Can't hear television: Personal listening device, closed captioning.

Can't read small print: Scanner with electronic voice output, print enlargement system, magnifying glass holder.

Can't see activites: TV magnifier, large game cards, large playing game pieces, talking games.

Can't hold books: Books on tape, book holder, scanner with voice electronic voice output.

| Stand Magnifier | Giant Bingo Cards | Hearing Amplifier | Low Vision Scrabble |

These suggestions and example images are only a sampling of the possible assistive aids.

Other Health Issues Related to Aging

The eye is one of the most amazing organs in the body. The eyes blink about 9,400 times a day. They move about 100,000 times daily.[81] The eyes are like a small video camera. Light enters the eye through a hole in the iris, pupil, and then to the retina. Components of the eye can become diseased, damaged, or weakened as we grow older. This is why the picture some people see is not clear, but distorted.

Visual impairments affect 18 percent of the older population, 16 percent of the women and 19 percent of the men. Those eighty-five and over, 33 percent reported having trouble seeing. Among those 65 and over in 2002 who reported trouble seeing, 16 percent reported having never had glaucoma, 16 percent reported never having macular degeneration, and 44 percent reported having cataracts in the previous 12 months.[82]

Components of the Human Eye

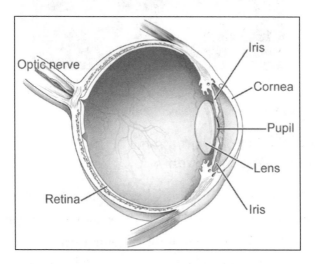

Photo courtesy of www.nih.gov

Blurry Vision, e.g., Cataract

The most common age-related eye condition is the cataract. It is a clouding of the normally clear and transparent lens of the eye that reduces passages of light. There is increased sensitivity to glare and everything looks hazy. Cataract surgery is recommended when the individual's vision has affected their ability to perform everyday tasks. Cataract surgery with a lens implant can restore vision to its former clarity.[83]

A scene as it might be viewed by a person with cataracts. Credit: National Eye Institute, National Institutes of Health Ref#: EDS05

Central Loss of Vision, e.g., Macular Degeneration

The leading cause of vision loss among older adults is macular degeneration. Macular degeneration is degenerative. It causes blurred and distorted central vision. The most common form among older adults is the "dry" form. There are approximately 15 million individuals in the United States that have age-related macular degeneration and about

16,000 new cases of macular degeneration are diagnosed each year. Scarring occurs in the macular area, the center of the retina, and thus creates difficulty in reading, writing, sewing, recognizing faces, and anything that requires detailed visual work. Currently there is no cure. Vision rehabilitation can be effective for learning new vision strategies and coping skills. Vision rehabilitation is a restorative service that includes low vision assessment, optical aid prescription, training in orientation and mobility, and training in activities of daily living.[84]

A scene as it might be viewed by a person with age-related macular degeneration. Credit: National Eye Institute, National Institutes of Health Ref#: EDS05

Peripheral Loss of Vision, e.g., Glaucoma

Some have called Glaucoma the "sneak thief of sight" because it affects the peripheral vision gradually and can be quite advanced before a problem is detected. Open-angle glaucoma affects about 2½ percent of the population over forty and increases with age. The condition is treatable and an annual glaucoma test performed by a vision specialist is recommended. Early diagnosis and treatment are very important in preventing additional vision loss. The central vision remains intact so reading is not usually a concern but orientation and mobility training are crucial.[85]

A scene as it might be viewed by a person with glaucoma. Credit: National Eye Institute, National Institutes of Health Ref#: EDS02

Blind Spots/Distorted Vision, e.g., Diabetic Retinopathy

Diabetic retinopathy is a result from a complication of diabetes. Retinopathy cannot be prevented but good control and management of diabetes can delay the onset. An individual's vision may fluctuate daily from nearly normal to distorted. Damaged blood vessels may leak fluid or blood in the eye, which causes retinal scars that distort the vision and/ or create blind spots. Controlling diabetes is imperative in minimizing its effects on vision.

A scene as it might be viewed by a person with
diabetic retinopathy. Credit: National Eye Institute,
National Institutes of Health Ref#: EDS04

Edentulism

The prevalence of edentulism, having no natural teeth, is higher—38 percent for people age eighty-five and over than for people sixty-five to seventy-four which is 24 percent. Socioeconomic differences appeared to make a difference with 46 percent of the older people with family income below the poverty line reported no natural teeth compared with 27 percent of the people above the poverty threshold.[86]

Rehabilitation Services

The disability rate is disproportionately high among the elderly. In many instances rehabilitation services can restore form or function after an illness or injury has occurred through the use of a variety of interventions directed at the disablement. Rehabilitation intervention services address the patient's ability to interact with the environment through restoration of full, modified independence, or assisted functions. Some diseases and illnesses pathology may affect the benefit gained from specific rehabilitation interventions or alter the way the interventions are presented. Interventions in rehabilitations services include (but are not limited to) exercise, prescriptions, adaptive techniques (modifications in the way an activity is performed), assistive technology (e.g., canes, walkers, wheelchairs), physical modalities (e.g., heat, cold, ultrasound), orthotic devices (braces, splints), and prosthesis (artificial limbs).

Exercise can help prevent disability and even reduce the extent of disability and counteract the adverse effects of immobility whether due to the systematic illness or trauma.[87] Despite physical limitations, adaptive techniques involving the modifying of a task are presented so that the patients can retain as much independence as possible. Being proficient with adaptive techniques allows the patients to interact with their environment in a more positive manner. Some adaptive techniques include learning to dress independently using one arm after having a stroke and losing the use of one arm, or the arthritic patient learning how to hold items properly so as not to stress the joints and taking rest breaks. There are numerous adaptive techniques and the use of them depends upon the illness and the skill level of the patient.

There are a number of rehabilitation specialists who assist the physician when the individual is receiving rehabilitation or therapy services. Some of the professionals involved are occupational therapists, physical therapists, speech-language therapists and nursing staff. Services are provided in a variety of settings including hospitals, sub-acute, outpatient, home care, and nursing homes. The treatment services that are provided by rehabilitation therapists are usually considered appropriate and reimbursed as long as the patient is making progress towards a measurable functional goal.

Other rehabilitation goals include shaping realistic goals in conjunction with the patient's goals and condition, educating patients about their potential for recovery, teaching self-care, advising patients, and care-givers. When function has been restored to an optimal or maximal level for the patient, a discharge plan is discussed and implemented.[88] Referral to a rehabilitation specialist can be a significant benefit when assistance is needed to eliminate, minimize, or modify the contextual factors that in many instances magnify or create disabilities. Individuals who are medically unstable may not be candidates for rehabilitation services at that time but may be in the future. This is determined by having the primary care provider reassess the patient regularly so that a proper determination for referring the patient for rehabilitation intervention services can be made. When the prognosis for recovery is encouraging, the negative effects of immobility are easier to prevent than remediate.

Putting Your House In Order

Believers have a home for the future. In John 14:3–4 we are promised that, "In my Father's house are many mansions: If it were not so, I would have told you. I go to prepare a place for you. And if I go and prepare a place for you, I will come again and receive you unto myself; that where I am that you may be also." We are not told the hour, day, or year, or when we will go to our Father's house, only that we will. But, what about now?

It is our duty to get our earthly house in order. Do you want to leave your family confused, fighting, and second guessing one another? It is difficult to think about wills, estate planning, and funerals because these things are all equated with death, sadness, and loss. Everyone, no matter what his or her age, should have a will. Estate planning would be even more beneficial. A will is a legal document specifying who the executor of the estate is and how an individual would like the transfer of their property and assets after their death. Estate planning not only includes having a will, but also letting family members know how you would like your funeral, financial, medical affairs, and other items handled as you have determined.

An attorney, CPA, or tax advisor who specializes in estate planning can assist in developing an estate plan. They can help in minimizing the taxable portion of your estate so that your heirs can gain the greatest benefit. This can be an eye-opening experience when you start adding up the value of your estate. Some of the items included when adding up your assets is your home, investments, retirement savings, and life insurance policies.

You know your desires and how you would like your affairs handled. Your wishes should be in a written legal document. This is a very stressful time for your loved ones. To help alleviate any arguments or displaced feelings it is best that everything is written down so that some of the unnecessary stress upon family members can be eliminated. They won't have to labor when making a decision, because you will have already made the decisions for them.

We specifically designed the CD *Putting Your House In Order: Before The Last Will And Testament,* so that all of your information is in one location. We've done all of the work. Just fill in the appropriate spaces and the end of each section can be tailored to meet an individual's specific situation.

Getting your affairs in order is not something that should be taken lightly or a responsibility that should be left to your loved ones. This is a time they will be grieving their loss and celebrating your homecoming.

Statistics on Aging and Mortality

Leading Causes of Death among Women Age Sixty-five and Over

	All races	White	African-American	Asian or Pacific Islander	American Indian	Hispanic
1	Diseases of heart	Diseases of heart	Diseases of heart	Diseases of heart	Diseases of heart	Diseases of heart
2	Malignant neoplasms	Malignant neoplasms	Malignant neoplasms	Malignant neoplasms	Malignant neoplasms	Malignant neoplasms
3	Cerebrovascular diseases	Cerebrovascular diseases	Cerebrovascular diseases	Cerebrovascular diseases	Cerebrovascular diseases	Cerebrovascular diseases
4	Chronic lower respiratory diseases	Chronic lower respiratory diseases	Diabetes mellitus	Diabetes mellitus	Diabetes mellitus	Diabetes mellitus
5	Alzheimer's disease	Alzheimer's disease	Nephritis, nephritic syndrome and nephrosis	Influenza and pneumonia	Chronic lower respiratory diseases	Influenza and pneumonia
6	Influenza and pneumonia	Influenza and pneumonia	Chronic lower respiratory diseases	Chronic lower respiratory diseases	Influenza and pneumonia	Chronic lower respiratory diseases
7	Diabetes mellitus	Diabetes mellitus	Influenza and pneumonia	Nephritis, nephritic syndrome and nephrosis	Accidents (unintentional injuries)	Alzheimer's disease
8	Nephritis, nephritic syndrome and nephrosis	Accidents (unintentional injuries)	Septicemia	Accidents (unintentional injuries)	Nephritis, nephritic syndrome and nephrosis	Nephritis, nephritic syndrome and nephrosis

Leading Causes of Death among Women Age Sixty-five and Over

All races	White	African-American	Asian or Pacific Islander	American Indian	Hispanic
9 Accidents (unintentional injuries)	Nephritis, nephritic syndrome and nephrosis	Alzheimer's disease	Essential (primary) hypertention and disease hypertensive renal disease	Alzheimer's disease	Accidents (unintentional injuries)
10 Septicemia	Septicemia	Essential (primary) hypertention and hypertensive renal disease	Alzheimer's disease	Chronic liver disease and cirrhosis	Septicemia

Reference population: This data refers to the resident population.

Source: Centers for Disease Control and Prevention, National Center for Health Statistics, National Vital Statistics System.

Leading Causes of Death among Men Age Sixty-five and Over

	All races	White	African-American	Asian or Pacific Islander	American Indian	Hispanic
1	Diseases of heart	Diseases of heart	Diseases of heart	Diseases of heart	Diseases of heart	Diseases of heart
2	Malignant neoplasms	Malignant neoplasms	Malignant neoplasms	Malignant neoplasms	Malignant neoplasms	Malignant neoplasms
3	Cerebrovascular diseases	Chronic lower respiratory diseases	Cerebrovascular diseases	Cerebrovascular diseases	Cerebrovascular diseases	Cerebrovascular diseases
4	Chronic lower respiratory diseases	Cerebrovascular diseases	Chronic lower respiratory diseases	Chronic lower respiratory diseases	Chronic lower respiratory diseases	Diabetes mellitus
5	Influenza and pneumonia	Influenza and pneumonia	Diabetes mellitus	Influenza and pneumonia	Diabetes mellitus	Chronic lower respiratory diseases
6	Diabetes mellitus	Diabetes mellitus	Nephritis, nephritic syndrome and nephrosis	Diabetes mellitus	Influenza and pneumonia	Influenza and pneumonia
7	Accidents (unintentional injuries)	Accidents (unintentional injuries)	Influenza and pneumonia	Accidents (unintentional injuries)	Accidents (unintentional injuries)	Nephritis, nephritic syndrome and nephrosis
8	Alzheimer's disease	Alzheimer's disease	Septicemia	Nephritis, nephritic syndrome and nephrosis	Nephritis, nephritic syndrome and nephrosis	Accidents (unintentional injuries)

Leading Causes of Death among Men Age Sixty-five and Over

	All races	White	African-American	Asian or Pacific Islander	American Indian	Hispanic
9	Nephritis, nephritic syndrome and nephrosis	Nephritis, nephritic syndrome and nephrosis	Accidents (unintentional injuries)	Septicemia	Septicemia	Chronic liver disease and cirrhosis
10	Septicemia	Septicemia	Essential (primary) hypertention and hypertensive renal disease	Aortic aneurysm and dissection	Chronic liver disease and cirrhosis	Septicemia

Reference population: This data refers to the resident population.

Source: Centers for Disease Control and Prevention, National Center for Health Statistics, National Vital Statistics System.

Chapter 4

A Final Thought

Christian counselors and other care-givers will inevitably come in contact with individuals differing in age, race, economic circumstances, educational backgrounds, and employment who will need assistance. These people carry deep hurt. Their anger, guilt, and hate have festered in their hearts—some for a long time. This is going to present an opportunity for counselors to use the Word of God. Christian care-givers can bring a message of salvation as they bring practical help on emotional, relational, and physical levels. Some counselees will have chosen to ignore the Word because of a hardened heart, but will now be thirsting for His Word. It is now time for the harvest described in John 4:35, "… lift up your eyes, and look on the fields; for they are white already to harvest."

Psalm 139:14 says, "We are fearfully and wonderfully made." We are as much the same as we are unique because we are all children of God. Christian counselors, health care professionals, and other care-givers who choose to specialize in working with aging issues, seniors, and their families have truly taken on a ministry that will heal the hurt of many. The more we stay abreast of issues, the more help we can provide—just as in any other area of counseling and health care. This hard work and effort can provide infinite healing and comfort for clients.

This area of counseling is not for everyone. Counselors who do not specialize in this area should refer counselees to someone who does. This can lift a deep burden off of the counselees' backs. The counselee will know there is hope and someone to help them.

There is one thing that we all have in common; we are all aging. Years ago, Flip Wilson, the television comedian, was known for saying that "if we had our entire lives to live over again we would probably not have the strength."[89] Hopefully we have lived life to its fullest. Carl Sandburg expressed his feeling about life by saying:

> *Life is like an onion:*
> *you peel it off*
> *one layer at a time,*
> *And sometimes you weep.*[90]

Respect for the individual is paramount, just because someone is old, hard of hearing, has dementia, or becomes physically disabled there is no reason to treat them like they don't have any feelings or worth. Even when a person needs assistance with activities of daily living, the assistance can be done with dignity. The following poem is a reminder about dignity and respect for the elderly by Shel Silverstein.

The Little Boy and the Old Man

Said the little boy,
"Sometimes I drop my spoon."
Said the old man
"I do that too."
The little boy whispered,
"I wet my pants."
"I do that too," laughed the little old man.
Said the little boy,
"I often cry."
The old man nodded,
"So do I."
"But worst of all," said the boy,
"It seems as if grown-ups don't pay attention to me."
And he felt the warmth of a wrinkled old hand.
"I know what you mean," said the little old man.[91]

If we do nothing more than remind those that we come into contact with to be respectful and treat the elderly with dignity, we will have solved many concerns and problems. Whether we want to believe it or not we will be old one day. How society is instructed and allowed to treat those in their golden years—our senior saints today—is only a taste of what our golden days will have in store for us. When we lose respect for our elderly we have lost our reverence for life.

As compassionate, empathetic, loving care-givers, we help make sure that a genuine respect—an active reverence—for every individual and the gift of life they've been given, is preserved in our minds, our hearts, our hands, and our world.

APPENDICES

Appendix A

A Glossary of Health Care Terms and Concepts

The following definitions explain terms and commonly used acronyms in this study and the health care industry. This information is presented so that the counselor and those involved can have a working knowledge of industry terminology. The counselor can explain the general processes and answer questions more accurately and informatively when he has a better understanding of the terminology and process involved.

Abuse (Personal)—When a person does something on purpose that causes mental or physical harm or pain to another.

Activities of Daily Living (ADLs)—Includes the self maintenance task of dressing, grooming, feeding, eating, mobility, communication, socialization, and sexual expression.

Admitting Physician—The doctor responsible for admitting a patient to a hospital or other inpatient health facility.

Advance Directives—A written document which formally states personal preferences for how medical decisions will be made if a person loses the ability to make them for him/herself. It may include a Living Will and a Durable Power of Attorney for health care.

Assisted Living—A type of living arrangement in which personal care services such as meals, housekeeping, transportation, and assistance with activities of daily living are available as needed to people who still live on their own in a residential facility. In most cases, the "assisted living" residents pay a regular monthly rent. Then, they typically pay additional fees for the services they get.

Care Plan—A written plan for health care. It tells what services a person prefers for reaching and keeping his or her best physical, mental, and social well-being.

Care-giver—A person who helps care for someone who is ill, disabled, or aged. Some care-givers are relatives or friends who volunteer their help. Some people provide professional care-giving services for a fee.

Durable Power of Attorney—A legal document that enables a person to designate someone else, called the attorney-in-fact, to act on his/her behalf in the event the document's author becomes disabled or incapacitated.

Geriatrics—The study of all aspects of aging including the physiological, psychological, economic, and sociological problems of the elderly.[92]

Home Health Care—Limited part-time or intermittent skilled nursing care and home health aide services, physical therapy, occupational therapy, speech-language therapy, medical social services, durable medical equipment (such as wheelchairs, hospital beds, oxygen, and walkers), medical supplies, and other services.

Homebound—Normally unable to leave the home unassisted. To be homebound means that leaving home takes considerable and taxing effort. A person may leave home for medical treatment or short, infrequent absences for non-medical reasons, such as a trip to the barber or to attend religious services. A need for adult day care doesn't keep a person from getting home health care.

Hospice—A special way of caring for people who are terminally ill, and for their family. This care includes physical care and counseling. Hospice care is covered under Medicare Part A (Hospital Insurance).

Living Wills—Legal document also known as a medical directive or advance directive. It states your wishes regarding life support or other medical treatment in certain circumstances, usually when death is imminent.

Long-Term Care Survey—An evaluation process by which a nursing home is inspected and evaluated to determine if they are meeting state and federal regulations.

Medicaid—A joint federal and state program that helps with medical costs for some people with low incomes and limited resources. Medicaid programs vary from state to state, but most health care costs are covered if you qualify for both Medicare and Medicaid.

Medicare—The federal health insurance program for: people sixty-five years of age or older, certain younger people with disabilities, and people with End-Stage Renal Disease (permanent kidney failure with dialysis or a transplant, sometimes called ESRD).

Nursing Home—A residence that provides a variety of services such as a room, meals, recreational activities, assistance with activities of daily living, and protection/supervision to residents. Nursing homes are licensed by the state and are required to follow state and federal regulations. Some nursing homes specialize in areas such as Alzheimer's disease, pain management, incontinence training, and cardiac rehab.

Occupational Therapy—A rehabilitation specialty that is provided by a licensed individual. The Occupational Therapist works with individuals with varying disabilities. The therapist may help the individual regain function, self feeding, oral hygiene, upper body strengthening, dressing/

bathing skills, visual/perceptual coordination, splinting, and adaptive equipment.

Ombudsman—Visits the nursing home on a regular basis. It is their job to mediate disputes, investigate complaints, and be an advocate for residents.

Physical Therapy—A rehabilitation specialty that is provided by a licensed individual. The Physical Therapist may work with an individual depending upon the diagnosis to help them regain functional abilities in walking, getting in/out of bed, strength, balance, gross motor skills, endurance and improve safety skills.

Range of Motion—The arc of motion which a joint passes through. ROM measurements can help a therapist determine appropriate treatment goals and current range of motion degrees.

Respiratory Services—Services provided to an individual who might have breathing disorders or breathing difficulties. Some of the areas respiratory services are provided are aerosol therapy, delivering oxygen therapy and exercises in breathing retraining.

Speech Language Pathologist—A rehabilitation specialty that is provided by a licensed individual. The Speech Language Pathologist assists individuals with varying disabilities. Some of the areas they assist individuals who have difficulties are chewing, swallowing, speech, comprehension, communications, and memory loss.

Appendix B

Abbreviations and Acronyms related to Aging and Health Care

ADLs: Activities of Daily Living

ADON: Assistant Director of Nursing

CNA: Certified Nursing Assistant

COTA: Certified Occupational Therapy Assistant

DON: Director of Nursing

LTC: Long-Term Care Facility

OT: Occupational Therapist

PT: Physical Therapist

PTA: Physical Therapy Assistant

ROM: Range of Motion

RT: Respiratory Therapist

SLP: Speech Language Pathologist

SNF: Skilled Nursing Facility

Appendix C

Legal Document Resources

The National Hospice and Palliative Care Organization has given the author permission to use the following forms in his book with the understanding that their copyright is reserved and these documents are offered only as examples for informational purposes. *Reproduction and distribution by an organization or organized group without the written permission of the National Hospice and Palliative Care Organization is expressly forbidden.*

GEORGIA
Advance Directive
Planning for Important Healthcare Decisions

Caring Connections
1731 King St., Suite 100, Alexandria, VA 22314
www.caringinfo.org
800/658-8898

Caring Connections, a program of the National Hospice and Palliative Care Organization (NHPCO), is a national consumer engagement initiative to improve care at the end of life.

Caring Connections tracks and monitors all state and federal legislation and significant court cases related to end-of-life care to ensure that our advance directives are up to date.

It's About How You LIVE

It's About How You LIVE is a national community engagement campaign encouraging individuals to make informed decisions about end-of-life care and services. The campaign encourages people to:

Learn about options for end-of-life services and care
Implement plans to ensure wishes are honored
Voice decisions to family, friends and healthcare providers
Engage in personal or community efforts to improve end-of-life care

Visit www.caringinfo.org to learn more about the LIVE campaign, obtain free resources, or join the effort to improve community, state and national end-of-life care.

If you would like to make a contribution to help support our work, please visit www.nationalhospicefoundation.org/donate. Contributions to national hospice programs can also be made through the Combined Health Charities or the Combined Federal Campaign by choosing #11241.

1

Your Advance Care Planning Packet

2

Using these materials

BEFORE YOU BEGIN

1. Check to be sure that you have the materials for each state in which you could receive healthcare.

2. These materials include:
   - Instructions for preparing your advance directive.
   - Your state-specific advance directive forms, which are the pages with the gray instruction bar on the left side.

PREPARING TO COMPLETE YOUR ADVANCE DIRECTIVE

3. Read the HIPAA Privacy Rule Summary on page 4.

4. Read all the instructions, on pages 7 through 8, as they will give you specific information about the requirements in your state.

5. Refer to the Glossary located in Appendix A if any of the terms are unclear.

ACTION STEPS

6. You may want to photocopy these forms before you start so you will have a clean copy if you need to start over.

7. When you begin to fill out the forms, refer to the gray instruction bars - they will guide you through the process.

8. Talk with your family, friends, and physicians about your advance directive. Be sure the person you appoint to make decisions on your behalf understands your wishes.

9. Once the form is completed and signed, photocopy the form and give it to the person you have appointed to make decisions on your behalf, your family, friends, healthcare providers and/or faith leaders so that the form is available in the event of an emergency.

If you have questions or need guidance in preparing your advance directive or about what you should do with it after you have completed it, please refer to the state-specific contacts for Legal & End-of-Life Care Resources Pertaining to Healthcare Advance Directives, located in Appendix B.

3

Summary of the HIPAA Privacy Rule

HIPAA is a federal law that gives you rights over your health information and sets rules and limits on who can look at and receive your health information.

Your Rights

You have the right to:
- Ask to see and get a copy of your health records.
- Have corrections added to your health information.
- Receive a notice that tells you how your health information may be used and shared.
- Decide if you want to give your permission before your health information can be used or shared for certain purposes, such as marketing.
- Get a report on when and why your health information was shared for certain purposes.

If you believe your rights are being denied or your health information isn't being protected, you can:
- File a complaint with your provider or health insurer, or
- File a complaint with the U.S. Government.

You also have the right to ask your provider or health insurer questions about your rights. You also can learn more about your rights, including how to file a complaint from the Web site at www.hhs.gov/ocr/hipaa/ or by calling 1-866-627-7748.

Who Must Follow this Law?

- Doctors, nurses, pharmacies, hospitals, clinics, nursing homes, and many other healthcare providers.
- Health insurance companies, HMOs, most employer group health plans.
- Certain government programs that pay for healthcare, such as Medicare and Medicaid.

What Information is Protected?

- Information your doctors, nurses, and other healthcare providers put in your medical record.
- Conversations your doctor has had about your care or treatment with nurses and other healthcare professionals.
- Information about you in your health insurer's computer system.
- Billing information about you from your clinic/healthcare provider's records.
- Most other health information about you, held by those who must follow this law.

4

Summary of the HIPAA Privacy Rule (continued)

Providers and health insurers who are required to follow this law must keep your information private by:

- Teaching the people who work for them how your information may and may not be used and shared,
- Taking appropriate and reasonable steps to keep your health information secure.

To make sure that your information is protected in a way that does not interfere with your healthcare, your information can be used and shared in the following instances:

- For your treatment and care coordination,
- To pay doctors and hospitals for your healthcare,
- With your family, relatives, friends or others you identify who are involved with your healthcare or your healthcare bills, unless you object,
- To protect the public's health, such as reporting when the flu is in your area, or
- To make required reports to the police, such as reporting gunshot wounds.

Your health information cannot be used or shared without your written permission unless this law allows it. For example, without your authorization, your provider generally cannot:

- Give your information to your employer,
- Use or share your information for marketing or advertising purposes, or
- Share private notes about your mental health counseling sessions.

5

144

INTRODUCTION TO YOUR GEORGIA ADVANCE DIRECTIVE FOR HEALTHCARE

This packet contains one legal document, the Georgia Advance Directive for Healthcare, that protects your right to refuse medical treatment you do not want or to request treatment you do want, in the event you lose the ability to make decisions yourself. The form contains three parts, any number of which may be filled out, and a fourth signature page that must be filled out for any of the three preceding parts to be effective.

1. Part One: **Healthcare Agent**. This allows you to choose someone to make healthcare decisions for you when you cannot (or do not want to) make healthcare decisions for yourself. You may also have your healthcare agent make decisions for you after your death with respect to an autopsy, organ donation, body donation, and final disposition of your body.

2. Part Two: **Treatment Preferences**. This part allows you to state your treatment preferences if you are (1) unable to communicate your treatment preferences, _and_ (2) you either have a terminal condition or are in a state of permanent unconsciousness. This part is optional. If you also have a healthcare agent, then your agent is authorized to make all decisions discussed in Part Two, but will be guided by your written Treatment Preferences as well as the other factors listed in section 4 of Part One.

3. Part Three: **Guardianship**. This part allows you to nominate a person to be your guardian should one ever be needed.

Note: These documents will be legally binding only if the person completing them is a competent adult (at least 18 years old).

6

GEORGIA DURABLE POWER OF ATTORNEY FOR HEALTHCARE

Whom should I appoint as my agent?

Your agent is the person you appoint to make decisions about your medical care if you become unable to make those decisions yourself. Your agent can be a family member or a close friend whom you trust to make serious decisions. The person you name as your agent should clearly understand your wishes and be willing to accept the responsibility of making medical decisions for you.

No physician or healthcare provider may act as your agent if he or she is directly involved in your healthcare.

You can appoint a second and third person as your alternate agent(s). The alternate will step in if the first person you name as agent is unable, unwilling or unavailable to act for you.

How do I make my Georgia Healthcare Agent legal?

The law requires that you sign your document, or direct another to sign it in your presence and at your express direction, in the presence of two witnesses who must be at least 18 years of age and of sound mind.

Neither witness can be a person who is any of the following: (1) is your healthcare agent; (2) will knowingly inherit anything from you or otherwise gain a financial benefit from your death; or (3) is directly involved in your healthcare.

Not more than one witness can be an employee, agent, or medical staff member of the healthcare facility in which you are receiving healthcare.

Note: You do not need to notarize your Georgia Advance Directive for Healthcare.

Should I add personal instructions to my Treatment Preferences document?

You can add personal instructions in section 8, "Additional instructions." For example, you may want to state your treatment preferences regarding medications to fight infection, surgery, amputation, blood transfusion, or kidney dialysis. You may also want to state your specific preferences regarding pain relief.

Understanding that you cannot foresee everything that could happen to you after you can no longer communicate your treatment preferences, you may want to provide guidance to your healthcare agent (if you have selected a healthcare agent in PART ONE) about following your treatment preferences and what you consider to be an acceptable "quality of life." One of the strongest reasons for naming an agent is to have someone who can respond flexibly as your medical situation changes and deal with situations that you did not foresee.

7

GEORGIA DURABLE POWER OF ATTORNEY FOR HEALTHCARE (CONTINUED)

What if I change my mind?
Revocation
You may revoke your Georgia Advance Directive for Healthcare at any time, regardless of your mental or physical condition, by:

- obliterating, burning, tearing, or otherwise destroying your document,
- signing and dating a written revocation or directing another person to do so (if you are receiving healthcare in a healthcare facility, the revocation must be communicated to your attending physician) , or
- orally revoking your document in the presence of a witness, at least 18 years of age, who must sign and date a written confirmation of your revocation within 30 days (if you are receiving healthcare in a healthcare facility, the revocation must be communicated to your attending physician).

Change in Marital Status
If you get married after completing the form for Power of Attorney for Healthcare and you have not named your spouse as your agent, your marriage automatically revokes the power of your agent. If you have appointed your spouse as your agent and your marriage ends, your agent's power is automatically revoked.

What other important facts should I know?
Pregnancy
If you are a woman and would like your Treatment Preferences regarding withholding or withdrawal of life-sustaining procedures, nourishment, or hydration to be honored even if you are pregnant, you must initial the statement in section 9 of the Advance Directive for healthcare form.

State law requires that before honoring a pregnant patient's Treatment Preferences, the attending physician must first determine whether the fetus is viable. If the fetus is viable, your Treatment Preferences will not be honored, even if you initial section 9.

Guardianship
Part III of your Advance Directive provides space where you can nominate someone to serve as your guardian if there should come a time when you need a court-appointed guardian. Unless a court specifies otherwise, your guardian has no power to make any personal or healthcare decisions granted to your agent under your Advance Directive for Healthcare.

8

GEORGIA ADVANCE DIRECTIVE FOR HEALTHCARE – PAGE 1 OF 9

NOTICE: The purpose of this Healthcare Agent form is to give the person you designate (your agent) broad powers to make healthcare decisions for you. Such decisions include the power to require, consent to, or withdraw any type of personal care or medical treatment for any physical or mental condition and to admit you to or discharge you from any hospital, home, or other institution. Such decisions do NOT include psychosurgery, sterilization, or involuntary hospitalization or treatment covered by Title 37 of the Official Code of Georgia Annotated.

The Healthcare Agent form does NOT impose a duty on your agent to exercise granted powers or to assume responsibility for your healthcare. However, when your agent does exercise granted powers, your agent will have to use due care to act for your benefit and in accordance with the terms of the Advance Directive for Healthcare.

Your healthcare agent may exercise the granted powers throughout your lifetime, even after you become disabled, incapacitated, or incompetent, until any of the following occur: (1) you expressly limit the duration of the granted powers in the Healthcare Agent form below; (2) you revoke the granted powers; or (3) a court acting on your behalf terminates the agent, which it may do if it finds your agent is acting improperly.

IF THERE IS ANYTHING ABOUT THIS FORM THAT YOU DO NOT UNDERSTAND, YOU SHOULD ASK A LAWYER TO EXPLAIN IT TO YOU.

9

GEORGIA ADVANCE DIRECTIVE FOR HEALTH CARE - PAGE 2 OF 9

By: _____
(Print Name)

Date of Birth: _____
(Month/Day/Year)

PART ONE: HEALTH CARE AGENT

(1) HEALTH CARE AGENT

I select the following person as my health care agent to make health care

decisions for me:

Name: _____

Address: _____

_____

Telephone Numbers: _____
(Home, Work, and Mobile)

(2) BACK-UP HEALTH CARE AGENT

*[**This section is optional.** PART ONE will be effective even if this section is left blank.]*

If my health care agent cannot be contacted in a reasonable time period and cannot be located with reasonable efforts or for any reason my health care agent is unavailable or unable or unwilling to act as my health care agent, then I select the following, each to act successively in the order named, as my back-up health care agent(s):

Name: _____

Address: _____

_____

Telephone Numbers: _____
(Home, Work, and Mobile)

Name: _____

Address: _____

_____

Telephone Numbers: _____
(Home, Work, and Mobile)

10

Aging Grace

(3) GENERAL POWERS OF HEALTH CARE AGENT

My health care agent will make health care decisions for me when I am unable to make my health care decisions or I choose to have my health care agent make my health care decisions. My health care agent will have the same authority to make any health care decision that I could make.

My health care agent's authority includes, for example, the power to:
- Admit me to or discharge me from any hospital, skilled nursing facility, hospice, or other health care facility or service;
- Request, consent to, withhold, or withdraw any type of health care; and
- Contract for any health care facility or service for me, and to obligate me to pay for these services (and my health care agent will not be financially liable for any services or care contracted for me or on my behalf).

My health care agent will be my personal representative for all purposes of federal or state law related to privacy of medical records (including the Health Insurance Portability and Accountability Act of 1996) and will have the same access to my medical records that I have and can disclose the contents of my medical records to others for my ongoing health care.

My health care agent may accompany me in an ambulance or air ambulance if in the opinion of the ambulance personnel protocol permits a passenger and my health care agent may visit or consult with me in person while I am in a hospital, skilled nursing facility, hospice, or other health care facility or service if its protocol permits visitation.

My health care agent may present a copy of this advance directive for health care in lieu of the original and the copy will have the same meaning and effect as the original.

I understand that under Georgia law:
- My health care agent may refuse to act as my health care agent;
- A court can take away the powers of my health care agent if it finds that my health care agent is not acting properly; and
- My health care agent does not have the power to make health care decisions for me regarding psychosurgery, sterilization, or treatment or involuntary hospitalization for mental or emotional illness, mental retardation, or addictive disease.

(4) GUIDANCE FOR HEALTH CARE AGENT

When making health care decisions for me, my health care agent should think about what action would be consistent with past conversations we have had, my treatment preferences as expressed in PART TWO (if I have filled out PART TWO), my religious and other beliefs and values, and how I have handled medical and other important issues in the past. If what I would decide is still unclear, then my health care agent should make decisions for me that my health care agent believes are in my best interest, considering the benefits, burdens, and risks of my current circumstances and treatment options.

11

Legal Document Resources

(5) POWERS OF HEALTH CARE AGENT AFTER DEATH

(A) AUTOPSY
My health care agent will have the power to authorize an autopsy of my body unless I have limited my health care agent's power by initialing below.

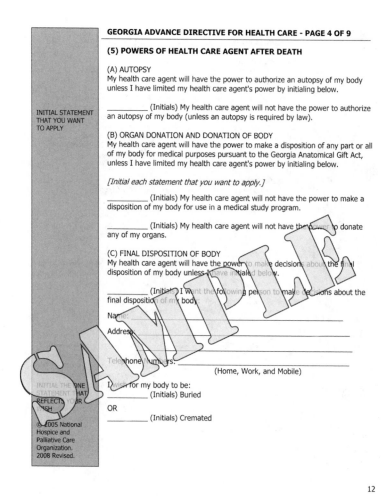

_____ (Initials) My health care agent will not have the power to authorize an autopsy of my body (unless an autopsy is required by law).

(B) ORGAN DONATION AND DONATION OF BODY
My health care agent will have the power to make a disposition of any part or all of my body for medical purposes pursuant to the Georgia Anatomical Gift Act, unless I have limited my health care agent's power by initialing below.

[Initial each statement that you want to apply.]

_____ (Initials) My health care agent will not have the power to make a disposition of my body for use in a medical study program.

_____ (Initials) My health care agent will not have the power to donate any of my organs.

(C) FINAL DISPOSITION OF BODY
My health care agent will have the power to make decisions about the final disposition of my body unless I have initialed below.

_____ (Initials) I want the following person to make decisions about the final disposition of my body:

Name: _____

Address: _____
_____

Telephone Numbers: _____
(Home, Work, and Mobile)

I wish for my body to be:
_____ (Initials) Buried
OR
_____ (Initials) Cremated

INITIAL STATEMENT THAT YOU WANT TO APPLY

INITIAL THE ONE STATEMENT THAT REFLECTS YOUR WISH

© 2005 National Hospice and Palliative Care Organization. 2008 Revised.

12

PART TWO: TREATMENT PREFERENCES

[PART TWO will be effective only if you are unable to communicate your treatment preferences after reasonable and appropriate efforts have been made to communicate with you about your treatment preferences. PART TWO will be effective even if PART ONE is not completed. If you have not selected a health care agent in PART ONE, or if your health care agent is not available, then PART TWO will provide your physician and other health care providers with your treatment preferences. If you have selected a health care agent in PART ONE, then your health care agent will have the authority to make all health care decisions for you regarding matters covered by PART TWO. Your health care agent will be guided by your treatment preferences and other factors described in Section (4) of PART ONE.]

(6) CONDITIONS

PART TWO will be effective if I am in any of the following conditions:

[Initial each condition in which you want PART TWO to be effective.]

_____ (Initials) A terminal condition, which means I have an incurable or irreversible condition that will result in my death in a relatively short period of time.

_____ (Initials) A state of permanent unconsciousness, which means I am in an incurable or irreversible condition in which I am not aware of myself or my environment and I show no behavioral response to my environment.

My condition will be certified in writing after personal examination by my attending physician and a second physician in accordance with currently accepted medical standards.

(7) TREATMENT PREFERENCES

[State your treatment preference by initialing (A), (B), or (C). If you choose (C), state your additional treatment preferences by initialing one or more of the statements following (C). You may provide additional instructions about your treatment preferences in the next section. You will be provided with comfort care, including pain relief, but you may also want to state your specific preferences regarding pain relief in the next section.]

If I am in any condition that I initialed in Section (6) above and I can no longer communicate my treatment preferences after reasonable and appropriate efforts have been made to communicate with me about my treatment preferences, then:

13

GEORGIA ADVANCE DIRECTIVE FOR HEALTH CARE - PAGE 6 OF 9

(A) _____ (Initials) Try to extend my life for as long as possible, using all medications, machines, or other medical procedures that in reasonable medical judgment could keep me alive. If I am unable to take nutrition or fluids by mouth, then I want to receive nutrition or fluids by tube or other medical means.

OR

(B) _____ (Initials) Allow my natural death to occur. I do not want any medications, machines, or other medical procedures that in reasonable medical judgment could keep me alive but cannot cure me. I do not want to receive nutrition or fluids by tube or other medical means except as needed to provide pain medication.

OR

(C) _____ (Initials) I do not want any medications, machines, or other medical procedures that in reasonable medical judgment could keep me alive but cannot cure me, except as follows:
[Initial each statement that you want to apply to option (C).]

_____ (Initials) If I am unable to take nutrition by mouth, I want to receive nutrition by tube or other medical means.

_____ (Initials) If I am unable to take fluids by mouth, I want to receive fluids by tube or other medical means.

_____ (Initials) If I need assistance to breathe, I want to have a ventilator used.

_____ (Initials) If my heart or pulse has stopped, I want to have cardiopulmonary resuscitation (CPR) used.

(8) ADDITIONAL STATEMENTS
[This section is optional. PART TWO will be effective even if this section is left blank. This section allows you to state additional treatment preferences, to provide additional guidance to your health care agent (if you have selected a health care agent in PART ONE), or to provide information about your personal and religious values about your medical treatment. For example, you may want to state your treatment preferences regarding medications to fight infection, surgery, amputation, blood transfusion, or kidney dialysis. Understanding that you cannot foresee everything that could happen to you after you can no longer communicate your treatment preferences, you may want to provide guidance to your health care agent (if you have selected a health care agent in PART ONE) about following your treatment preferences. You may want to state your specific preferences regarding pain relief.]

14

GEORGIA ADVANCE DIRECTIVE FOR HEALTH CARE - PAGE 7 OF 9

(9) IN CASE OF PREGNANCY
[PART TWO will be effective even if this section is left blank.]

I understand that under Georgia law, PART TWO generally will have no force and effect if I am pregnant unless the fetus is not viable and I indicate by initialing below that I want PART TWO to be carried out.

_____ (Initials) I want PART TWO to be carried out if my fetus is not viable.

PART THREE: GUARDIANSHIP

(10) GUARDIANSHIP
*[**PART THREE is optional.** This advance directive for health care will be effective even if PART THREE is left blank. If you wish to nominate a person to be your guardian in the event a court decides that a guardian should be appointed, complete PART THREE. A court will appoint a guardian for you if the court finds that you are not able to make significant responsible decisions for yourself regarding your personal support, safety, or welfare. A court will appoint the person nominated by you if the court finds that the appointment will serve your best interest and welfare. If you have selected a health care agent in PART ONE, you may (but are not required to) nominate the same person to be your guardian. If your health care agent and guardian are not the same person, your health care agent will have priority over your guardian in making your health care decisions, unless a court determines otherwise.]*

[State your preference by initialing (A) or (B). Choose (A) only if you have also completed PART ONE.]
(A) _____ (Initials) I nominate the person serving as my health care agent under PART ONE to serve as my guardian.

OR

(B) _____ (Initials) I nominate the following person to serve as my guardian.
Name: _____
Address: _____

Telephone Numbers: _____
                              (Home, Work, and Mobile)

INITIAL

15

GEORGIA ADVANCE DIRECTIVE FOR HEALTH CARE - PAGE 8 OF 9

PART FOUR: EFFECTIVENESS AND SIGNATURES

This advance directive for health care will become effective only if I am unable or choose not to make or communicate my own health care decisions.

This form revokes any advance directive for health care, durable power of attorney for health care, health care proxy, or living will that I have completed before this date.

Unless I have initialed below and have provided alternative future dates or events, this advance directive for health care will become effective at the time I sign it and will remain effective until my death (and after my death to the extent authorized in Section (5) of PART ONE).

_____ (Initials) This advance directive for health care will become effective on or upon _____ and will terminate on or upon _____.

[You must sign and date or acknowledge signing and dating this form in the presence of two witnesses. Both witnesses must be of sound mind and must be at least 18 years of age, but the witnesses do not have to be together or present with you when you sign this form.

A witness:

- *Cannot be a person who was selected to be your health care agent or back-up health care agent in PART ONE;*
- *Cannot be a person who will knowingly inherit anything from you or otherwise knowingly gain a financial benefit from your death; or*
- *Cannot be a person who is directly involved in your health care.*

Only one of the witnesses may be an employee, agent, or medical staff member of the hospital, skilled nursing facility, hospice, or other health care facility in which you are receiving health care (but this witness cannot be directly involved in your health care).]

By signing below, I state that I am emotionally and mentally capable of making this advance directive for health care and that I understand its purpose and effect.

_____   _____
(Signature of Declarant)   (Date)

INITIAL

SIGN AND DATE

© 2005 National Hospice and Palliative Care Organization. 2008 Revised.

16

Aging Grace

GEORGIA ADVANCE DIRECTIVE FOR HEALTH CARE - PAGE 9 OF 9

WITNESS

The declarant signed this form in my presence or acknowledged signing this form to me. Based upon my personal observation, the declarant appeared to be emotionally and mentally capable of making this advance directive for health care and signed this form willingly and voluntarily.

SIGN AND DATE

_____   _____
(Signature of witness)   (Date)

Print Name: _____

Address: _____

_____   _____
(Signature of witness)   (Date)

Print Name: _____

Address: _____

_____

[This form does not need to be notarized.]

© 2005 National Hospice and Palliative Care Organization. 2008 Revised.

Courtesy of Caring Connections
1731 King St., Suite 100, Alexandria, VA 22314
www.caringinfo.org, 800/658-8898

17

You Have Filled Out Your Advance Directive, Now What?

1. Your Georgia Advance Directive for Healthcare is an important legal document. Keep the original signed document in a secure but accessible place. Do not put the original document in a safe deposit box or any other security box that would keep others from having access to them.

2. Give photocopies of the signed originals to your agent and alternate agents, doctor(s), family, close friends, clergy, and anyone else who might become involved in your healthcare. If you enter a nursing home or hospital, have photocopies of your documents placed in your medical records.

3. Be sure to talk to your agent and alternates, doctor(s), clergy, and family and friends about your wishes concerning medical treatment. Discuss your wishes with them often, particularly if your medical condition changes.

4. If you want to make changes to your documents after they have been signed and witnessed, you must complete new documents.

5. Remember, you can always revoke any of your Georgia documents.

6. Be aware that your Georgia documents will not be effective in the event of a medical emergency. Ambulance personnel are required to provide cardiopulmonary resuscitation (CPR) unless they are given a separate order that states otherwise. These orders, commonly called "non-hospital do-not-resuscitate orders," are designed for people whose poor health gives them little chance of benefiting from CPR. These orders must be signed by your physician and instruct ambulance personnel not to attempt CPR if your heart or breathing should stop.

   Currently not all states have laws authorizing non-hospital do-not-resuscitate orders. We suggest you speak to your physician for more information. **Caring Connections does not distribute these forms.**

18

Appendix A

Glossary

Advance directive - A general term that describes two kinds of legal documents, living wills and medical powers of attorney. These documents allow a person to give instructions about future medical care should he or she be unable to participate in medical decisions due to serious illness or incapacity. Each state regulates the use of advance directives differently.

Artificial nutrition and hydration – Artificial nutrition and hydration supplements or replaces ordinary eating and drinking by giving a chemically balanced mix of nutrients and fluids through a tube placed directly into the stomach, the upper intestine or a vein.

Brain death – The irreversible loss of all brain function. Most states legally define death to include brain death.

Capacity - In relation to end-of-life decision-making, a patient has medical decision making capacity if he or she has the ability to understand the medical problem and the risks and benefits of the available treatment options. The patient's ability to understand other unrelated concepts is not relevant. The term is frequently used interchangeably with competency but is not the same. Competency is a legal status imposed by the court.

Cardiopulmonary resuscitation - Cardiopulmonary resuscitation (CPR) is a group of treatments used when someone's heart and/or breathing stops. CPR is used in an attempt to restart the heart and breathing. It may consist only of mouth-to-mouth breathing or it can include pressing on the chest to mimic the heart's function and cause blood to circulate. Electric shock and drugs also are used frequently to stimulate the heart.

Do-Not-Resuscitate (DNR) order - A DNR order is a physician's written order instructing healthcare providers not to attempt cardiopulmonary resuscitation (CPR) in case of cardiac or respiratory arrest. A person with a valid DNR order will not be given CPR under these circumstances. Although the DNR order is written at the request of a person or his or her family, it must be signed by a physician to be valid. A non-hospital DNR order is written for individuals who are at home and do not want to receive CPR.

Emergency Medical Services (EMS): A group of governmental and private agencies that provide emergency care, usually to persons outside of healthcare facilities; EMS personnel generally include paramedics, first responders and other ambulance crew.

Healthcare agent: The person named in an advance directive or as permitted under state law to make healthcare decisions on behalf of a person who is no longer able to make medical decisions.

19

Hospice - Considered to be the model for quality, compassionate care for people facing a life-limiting illness or injury, hospice and palliative care involve a team-oriented approach to expert medical care, pain management, and emotional and spiritual support expressly tailored to the person's needs and wishes. Support is provided to the persons loved ones as well.

Intubation- Refers to "endotracheal intubation" the insertion of a tube through the mouth or nose into the trachea (windpipe) to create and maintain an open airway to assist breathing.

Life-sustaining treatment - Treatments (medical procedures) that replace or support an essential bodily function (may also be called life support treatments). Life-sustaining treatments include cardiopulmonary resuscitation, mechanical ventilation, artificial nutrition and hydration, dialysis, and other treatments.

Living will - A type of advance directive in which an individual documents his or her wishes about medical treatment should he or she be at the end of life and unable to communicate. It may also be called a "directive to physicians", "healthcare declaration," or "medical directive."

Mechanical ventilation - Mechanical ventilation is used to support or replace the function of the lungs. A machine called a ventilator (or respirator) forces air into the lungs. The ventilator is attached to a tube inserted in the nose or mouth and down into the windpipe (or trachea).

Medical power of attorney - A document that allows an individual to appoint someone else to make decisions about his or her medical care if he or she is unable to communicate. This type of advance directive may also be called a healthcare proxy, durable power of attorney for healthcare or appointment of a healthcare agent. The person appointed may be called a healthcare agent, surrogate, attorney-in-fact or proxy.

Palliative care - A comprehensive approach to treating serious illness that focuses on the physical, psychological, spiritual, and existential needs of the patient. Its goal is to achieve the best quality of life available to the patient by relieving suffering, and controlling pain and symptoms.

Power of attorney – A legal document allowing one person to act in a legal matter on another's behalf regarding financial or real estate transactions.

Respiratory arrest: The cessation of breathing - an event in which an individual stops breathing. If breathing is not restored, an individual's heart eventually will stop beating, resulting in cardiac arrest.

20

Surrogate decision-making - Surrogate decision-making laws allow an individual or group of individuals (usually family members) to make decisions about medical treatments for a patient who has lost decision-making capacity and did not prepare an advance directive. A majority of states have passed statutes that permit surrogate decision making for patients without advance directives.

Ventilator – A ventilator, also known as a respirator, is a machine that pushes air into the lungs through a tube placed in the trachea (breathing tube). Ventilators are used when a person cannot breathe on his or her own or cannot breathe effectively enough to provide adequate oxygen to the cells of the body or rid the body of carbon dioxide.

Withholding or withdrawing treatment - Forgoing life-sustaining measures or discontinuing them after they have been used for a certain period of time.

Appendix B

Legal & End-of-Life Care Resources Pertaining to Healthcare Advance Directives

LEGAL SERVICES

Georgia Senior Legal Hotline works with agencies and organizations to respond to the needs of the elderly.

Individuals 60 and older can get legal referrals and advice about most issues, including:
- Living Wills / Power of Attorney
- Medicare and Medicaid
- Civil issues and other non-criminal matters

This service is free for individuals over 60 with low to moderate incomes

For more information call toll free: 1-888-257-9519 or 404-657- 9915

OR

Visit their website for more information: http://www.atlantalegalaid.org/departments.htm

END-OF-LIFE SERVICES

The Georgia Department of Human Resources, Division of Aging Services administers a statewide system of services for senior citizens, their families and caregivers. The services are available to individuals 60 and older with low to moderate incomes.

Anyone over 60 can receive resources and services for, but not limited:
- Housing
- Legal assistance
- Personal home care
- Meals on Wheels
- Transportation and many other services

To locate the closest Area Agency on Aging (AAA):
Call toll free: 1-866-351-0001 or 404-818-6600

OR

Visit Your State's AAA Web site:
http://aging.dhr.georgia.gov/

22

Appendix D

Resources for Additional Research and Reading

Housing Options

Assisted Living Federation www.alfa.org
MyNursingHomes.com www.mynursinghomes.com
Medicare www.medicare.gov

Organizations

American Diabetes Assoc. www.diabetes.org
Arthritis Foundation www.arthritis.com
Alzheimers Association www.alz.com
American Society On Aging www.asaging.org

Books

Parent Care: Fear and Losses of the Elderly
    By R. Bathauer
Eldercare 911: Knowing when Your Parent Needs Help
    By S. Beeman
Aging Parents: When Mom & Dad Can't Live Alone Anymore
    By E. Weisheit

Health Information Web Sites

WebMD www.webmd.com
Mediconsult www.mediconsult.com
Reuters Health www.reutershealth.com

Bibliography

Anderson, Neil T. et al. *Christ Centered Therapy.* Grand Rapids, Michigan: Zondervan Publishing House, 2002.

Bathauer, Ruth M. *Parent Care: Fear and Losses of the Elderly.* USA: Regal Book, 1984.

Beerman, Susan and Rappaport-Musson, Judith. *Eldercare 911: The Caregiver's Complete Handbook for Making Decisions.* Amherst, New York: Prometheus Books, 2002.

Biegel, Leonard. *Physical Fitness and the Older Person: A Guide to Exercise for Health Care Professionals.* Rockville, MD: Aspen Publication, 1984.

Bingham, Caroline. *Human Body.* New York, New York: DK Publishing, Inc., 2003.

Bonder, Bette R., and Wagner, Marilyn B. *Functional Performance In Older Adults.* Philadelphia, PA: F. A. Davis Company, 1994.

Bucher, L. (2004) *Advance Care Planning: Preference for Care at the End of Life.*

Christenson, Margaret A. *Aging in the Designed Environment*. Binghamton, New York: Haworth Press, 1990.

Davis, Ruth. *The Nursing Home Handbook*. Holbrook, Massachusetts: Adams Media Corporation, 2000.

Encyclopedia Britannia, *Eyes*, 1994.

Frankl, Viktor E. *Man's Search for Meaning*. New York, New York: Touchstone, 1962.

Gelhaus, L. (2004). *Boomers Prefer Aging At Home*. Provider Magazine, Vol.30. p.12&15.

Alma E. Guinness, ed., *ABC's of the Human Body*. USA: Reader's Digest, 1987.

Hirama, Haru. *Occupational Therapy Assistant: A Primer*. Baltimore, MD: Chess Publication, Inc. 1990.

Hiavochee Joe. P., *Keeping Young and Living Longer*. Los Angeles, CA: Sherbourne Press, 1972.

King James Version Bible

Lamson, Carl.C. and Petroff, Mark. *The Fundamentals of Stroke*. Health Library. Retrieved 7/5/2004, http://healthlibrary.healthology.com/focus_article.asp?b=heal thlibrary&f=healthyaing&...

Littauer, F., *Your Personality Tree*. Waco, Texas: Word
   Books, 1986.

Lynch, Eleanor W. and Hanson, Marci J. *Developing Cross-
   Cultural Competence* Baltimore, Maryland: Paul H.
   Publishing Co. 1992.

Mathy Mezey, ed. *The Encyclopedia of Elder Care*. Amherst,
   New York: Prometheus Books, 2004. Advance
   Directives-The National Hospice and Palliative Care
   Organization (2005). *Hospice & Palliative Care*.
   Retrieved 5/3/2005, http://www.nhpco.org/i4a/pages/
   Index.cfm?pageid=4415.

Merz, Beverly. (1992, October). *Why We Get Old*. Harvard
   Health Letter. 9-12.

New International Version of the Bible, (1978). New York
   Bible Society.

Old Age, (2005). Old Age. Retrieved 2/22/2005, http://
   www.realtime.net/wdoud/topics/oldage.html.

Older Americans 2004. U.S. Government Printing.
   Schomp, Virginia. *Aging Parent Handbook: The Baby
   Boomer Dilemma*. New York, New York: Harper
   Collins Publishers, 1997.

Shelly, Susan. *When It's Your Turn: Grown Children Caring for Aging Parents.* New York: Barnes & Nobles, 2002. Penny Smith, ed., *First Human Body Encyclopedia.* New York, New York: DK Publishing, Inc. 2003,

Taira, Ellen D. and Carlson, Jodi. *Aging in Place: Designing, Adapting, and Enhancing the Home Environment.* New York: Haworth Press, 2002. The FHA *Elder Care at Home* Chapter 25 "Understanding the Problems." Retrieved 7/5/2004. http://www.healthinaging.org/public_education/eldercare/2525.xml

U.S. Bureau of Census 2000, *Aging - American FactFinder* Retrieved 7/5/2004, http://factfinder.census.gov/jsp/saff/saffinfo.jsp?_pageID=tp2_agig

U.S. Department of Health and Human Services (2002). *What Is Assisted Living.* Retrieved 7/9/2004 http://www.alfa.org/public/articles/details.cfm?id=126

Weisheit, Eldon. *Aging Parents: When Mom & Dad Can't Live Alone Anymore.* Elgin, Illinois: Lion Publishing, 1994.

Notes

1. Bette R. Bonder, and Marilyn B. Wagner, *Functional Performance In Older Adults,* (Philadelphia, PA, 1994), p. 9.

2. Penny Smith, ed., First Human Body Encyclopedia, (New York, New York, 2003), p. 5.

3. Alma E. Guinness, ed., *ABC's Of The Human Body.* USA: Reader's Digest Books, (USA, 1987), p. 22.

4. Caroline Bingham. *Human Body.* (New York, New York: DK Publishing, Inc., 2003), p. 10.

5. Penny Smith, ed., *First Human Body Encyclopedia,* (New York, New York, 2003), p. 33.

6. Beverly Merz. (1992, October). *Why We Get Old.* Harvard Health Letter. 9-12.

7. Caroline Bingham. *Human Body.* (New York, New York: DK Publishing, Inc., 2003).

8. Caroline Bingham, *Human Body,* (New York, New York, 2003) p. 22.

9. Penny Smith, ed., *First Human Body Encyclopedia,* (New York, New York, 2003), p. 24.

10. Caroline Bingham, *Human Body,* (New York, New York, 2003) p. 17.

11. Beverly Merz. (1992, October). *Why We Get Old.* Harvard Health Letter. pp. 9-12.

12. Introduction to Healthy Aging, Partricia Bloom, MD http://healthlibrary.healthology.com/focus_article. asp?b=healthlibrary

13. Susan Shelly, *When It's Your Turn: Grown Children Caring for Aging Parents,* (New York, 2002), p. 103.

14. Margaret A. Christenson, *Aging in the Designed Environmen*t, (Binghamton, New York,1990), p. 10.

15. Mathy Mezey, ed., *The Encyclopedia of Elder Care,* (Amherst, New York, 2004), p. 73.

16. Ruth M. Bathauer, *Parent Care: Fear and Losses of the Elderly,* (USA, 1984), p. 99.

17. L. Gelhaus, (2004), *Boomers Prefer Aging At Home,* Provider Magazine, Vol.30. p.12&15.

18. Viktor E. Frankl, *Man's Search for Meaning,* (New York, New York, 1962).

19. Leonard Biegel, *Physical Fitness and the Older Person: A Guide to Exercise for Health Care Professionals, (*Rockville, MD, 1984), p. 30.

20. Joe P. Hiavochee, *Keeping Young and Living Longer*, (Los Angeles, CA, 1972), p. 129.

21. Federal Interagency Forum on Aging Related Statistics. *Older Americans 2004*: Key Indicators of Well-Being, Federal Interagency Forum on Aging Related Statistics Washington, DC U.S. Government Printing Office November 2004, pp. XIV, 34.

22. Mathy Mezey, ed., *The Encyclopedia of Elder Care,* (Amherst, New York, 2004), p. 586.

23. Ibid.

24. L. Bucher, *Advance Care Planning: Preference for Care at the End of Life,* (USA, 2005), p. 103.

25. Federal Interagency Forum on Aging Related Statistics.

26. Bette R. Bonder, and Marilyn B. Wagner, *Functional Performance In Older Adults,* (Philadelphia, PA, 1994), pp. 5, 9.

27. Ibid.

28. Federal Interagency Forum on Aging Related Statistics, p. 2.

29. Ibid, p. 3.

30. Ibid.

31. *Older Americans 2004.* U.S. Government Printing, p.3.

32. Federal Interagency Forum on Aging Related Statistics.

33. Ibid.

34. *Old Age,* (2005). Old Age. Retrieved 2/22/2005, http://www.realtime.net/~wdoud/topics/oldage.html.

35. Susan Beerman and Judith Rappaport-Musson, *Eldercare 911: The Caregiver's Complete Handbook for Making Decisions,* (Amherst, New York, 2002), p. 20.

36. Ibid, p. 37.

37. Ibid., p. 39.

38. Virginia Schomp, *Aging Parent Handbook: The Baby Boomer Dilemma,* (New York, New York, 1997), p. xv.

39. US CENSUS BUREAU Geographical Mobility http://www.census.gov/population/www/pop-profile/ geomob.html.

40. Littauer, F., *Your Personality Tree.* Waco, Texas: Word Books, 1986, pp. 232-235.

41. Mathy Mezey, ed., *The Encyclopedia of Elder Care,* (Amherst, New York, 2004), p. 9.

42. Developed by Thomas Holmes and Richard Rahe. Homes-Rahe Social Readjustment Rating Scale, Journal of Psychosomatic Research. Voll II, 1967.

43. An example of The Emergency Contact List is included in Chapter 3, Grace-Filled Solutions.

44. Margaret A. Christenson, *Aging in the Designed Environment,* (Binghamton, New York,1990), p. 55.

45. Additional suggestions for home modification and assistive living helps are available in Chapter 3, Grace-Filled Solutions.

46. See Chapter 3, Grace-Filled Solutions, for the "Home Safety & Modification Checklist.

47. Bette R. Bonder, and Marilyn B. Wagner, *Functional Performance In Older Adults,* (Philadelphia, PA, 1994), p. 16.

48. Ibid, p. 10.

49. Elenor W. Lynch, and Marci J. Hanson, *Developing Cross-Cultural Competence,* (Baltimore, Maryland, 1992), p. 3.

50. *Older Americans 2008* and *Older Americans 2004,* p. 22.

51. Neil T. Anderson, et al., *Christ Centered Therapy,* (Grand Rapids, Michigan, 2002), p. 135.

52. Florence Littauer, *Your Personality Tree* (Waco, Texas, 1986), p. 79.

53. *Older Americans 2004,* p. 24.

54. Ibid, p. 30.

55. Ibid.

56. Virginia Schomp, *Aging Parent Handbook: The Baby Boomer Dilemma,* (New York, New York,1997), pp. 45-46.

57. www.arthritis.com (accessed July 5, 2004).

58. *Older Americans 2004,* p. 24.

59. www.nia.nih.gov/alzheimers/alzheimersinformation/generalinfo/.

60. www.diabetes.org/about-diabetes.jsp (accessed July 5, 2004).

61. Carl C. Lamson, and Mark Petroff, T*he Fundamentals Of Stroke,* Health Library. (accessed July 5, 2004).

62. www.medicare.gov/Publications/Pubs/pdf/10116.pdf (accessed November 28, 2009).

63. *Older Americans 2008,* p. 25.

64. MetLife in cooperation with the National Alliance for Caregiving, *Since You Care*, (New York, New York, 2007).

65. *Older Americans 2004*, p. XIV.

66. *Older Americans 2008*, p. 20.

67. *Older Americans 2004*, p. 14.

68. L. Gelhaus, *Boomers Prefer Aging At Home*, Provider Magazine, 2004, Vol.30. p.12&15.

69. Ruth Davis, *The Nursing Home Handbook*, (Holbrook, Massachusetts,2000), p. 47.

70. Ellen D. Taira, and Jodi Carlson, Aging in Place: Designing, Adapting, and Enhancing the Home Environment, (New York, 2002), p. 77.

71. 53 Copyright © 2005 National Hospice and Palliative Care Organization. All rights reserved. Revised 2008. *Reproduction and distribution by an organization or organized group without the written permission of the National Hospice and Palliative Care Organization is expressly forbidden. Used with permission.* Forms and more info available at www.caringinfo.org/DownloadAdvanceDirective.htm

72. U.S. Bureau of Census 2000, *Aging - American FactFinder*, (accessed July 5, 2004), http://factfinder.census.gov/jsp/saff/saffinfo.jsp?_pageID=tp2_agig.

73. www.winaresort.com/blog/blog/tag/centerarians (accessed November 28, 2009).

74. Virginia Schomp, *Aging Parent Handbook: The Baby Boomer Dilemma*, (New York, New York, 1997), p. 56.

75. www.ahrq.gov.research/longtrm1hlm (accessed April 4, 2001).

76. www.aoa.gov/may2000/factsheets/growth.html (accessed April 4, 2001).

77. Ibid.

78. Adapted from Susan Beerman and Judith Rappaport-Musson, Eldercare 911: The Caregiver's Complete Handbook for Making Decisions, rev. ed (Amherst, NY: Prometheus Books, 2009), pp. 145-146.

79. Ellen D. Taira, and Jodi Carlson, *Aging in Place: Designing, Adapting, and Enhancing the Home Environment*, (New York, 2002), p. 1.

80. *Older Americans 2004*, p. 57.

81. *Eye Wonder Human Body, C Bingham.*

82. *Older Americans 2004.*

83. Ibid, p. 62–63.

84. Taira, Ellen D. and Carlson, Jodi. *Aging in Place: Designing, Adapting, and Enhancing the Home Environment.* New York: Haworth Press, 2002.

85. Ibid, p. 64.

86. *Older Americans 2004*, p. 25.

87. Mathy Mezey, ed., *The Encyclopedia of Elder Care*, (Amherst, New York, 2004), p.560.

88. Ibid, p. 562.

89. Ruth M. Bathauer, *Parent Care: Fear and Losses of the Elderly,* (USA, 1984), p. 31.

90. http://en.thinkexist.com/quotation/life_is_like_an_onion-you_peel_it_off_one_layer/183238.html (accessed November 8, 2009).

91. http://famouspoetsandpoems.com/poets/shel_silverstein/poems/14823 (accessed November 8, 2009).

92. Haru Hirama, *Occupational Therapy Assistant: A Primer,* (Baltimore, MD,1990), p. 285.

IF YOU'RE A FAN OF THIS BOOK, PLEASE TELL OTHERS...

- Write about *Aging Grace* on your blog, Twitter, MySpace, and Facebook page.

- Suggest *Aging Grace* to friends.

- When you're in a bookstore, ask them if they carry the book. The book is available through all major distributors so any bookstore that does not have *Aging Grace* in stock can easily order it.

- Write a positive review of *Aging Grace* on www.amazon.com.

- Send my publisher, HigherLife Publishing, suggestions on Web sites, conferences, and events you know of where this book could be offered at info@ahigherlife.com.

- Purchase additional copies to give away as gifts.

CONNECT WITH ME...

I am available for seminars on Aging. Please call (678) 720-5876 to schedule a seminar at your location or visit www.designsforaging.org for previously scheduled seminars.

In addition to the *Aging Grace—Advice for Pastors, Counselors, and Families of Aging Relatives* book, a CD of all necessary forms has been designed so that all of your information is in one location. The CD is entitled *Putting Your House In Order: Before The Last Will And Testament* and can be ordered by mail at P.O. Box 1986, Douglasville, GA 30133, by phone at (678) 720-5876 or by email at drrickcc@gmail.com.

You may also contact my publisher directly about the book or CD:

HigherLife Development Services, Inc.
400 Fontana Circle
Building 1 – Suite 105
Oviedo, Florida 32765
Phone: (407) 563-4806
Email: info@ahigherlife.com